이수영

2번이 정답인
수능기본
영단어 영문장

이²번이 정답인 수능기본 영단어 영문장

성근모 지음

지식공감 도서출판

이 책의 특징

우리말 문장에서 영단어의 의미를 유추하고
오답률 zero에 도전하는 단어 문제로
정확한 영단어 의미를 파악합니다.

우리말 문장을 영어문장으로 다시 정리하여
전체적인 우리말과 영어문장의 차이를 자연스럽게
이해할 수 있습니다.

TEST 복습과 묶음해석 연습을 통해 영단어·영문장을 마무리합니다.
TEST 복습과 묶음해석 연습에는 따로 정답지가 없습니다.
정답 확인을 위해 앞의 내용을 돌아보는 수고를 통해 실력을 한 번 더
다질 수 있는 기회가 되기 때문입니다.
또한, 사전을 찾아보는 습관을 키우기 위해 영단어 발음기호도 표기하지
않았습니다.

알찬 문장들입니다. 우리말 흐름을 먼저 잘 이해하고
영어문장을 통째로 외우면 최고!

CONTENTS

CONTENTS

이번이 정답인 **수**능기본 **영**단어

* **Archeologists**는 지난 다섯 달 동안 이 뼈를 복원하기 위해 작업을 해왔다.

➡ .... 친 단어의 뜻은?
 ① 고등학생들　　　　　② 고고학자들

Archeologists have worked to recover the bones for the past five months.

* 그의 **tomb**에는 대리석으로 만들어진 큰 관이 있다.

➡ .... 친 단어의 뜻은?
 ① 침대　　　　② 무덤

In his **tomb**, there is a big coffin made of marble.

> 과거분사구가 명사를
> 후치 수식합니다.

recover 복원하다, 회복하다　　bone 뼈　　coffin 관

✳ 고고학자들은 지금까지 이 지역에서 500개 이상의 무덤을 **have excavated**.

➡ .... 친 단어의 뜻은?
① 도굴해 왔다.   ② 발굴해 왔다.

Archeologists **have excavated** over 500 tombs at the site so far.

✳ 그는 위대한 **sculptor**이었으며 그의 대리석 조각인 '다비드상'은 역대 가장 유명한 조각품 중 하나이다.

➡ .... 친 단어의 뜻은?
① 이발사   ② 조각가

He was a great **sculptor** and his marble statue,
"David" is one of the most famous sculptures of all time.

"~ 중에 하나"인 one of 뒤에는
당연히 복수명사가 옵니다.

statue 조각(상)   sculpture 조각품, 조각하다

11

* 그녀는 해리포터 시리즈를 쓴 세계적으로 유명한 **author**이다.

➡ .... 친 단어의 뜻은?
   ① 남자   ② 작가

She is a world—famous **author** who wrote the Harry Potter series.

> 관계대명사 who 절이
> 앞 명사를 꾸며줍니다.

* **Metabolism**은 살아있는 세포 또는 유기체 안에서 발생하는 **화학적인** 과정이다.

➡ .... 친 단어의 뜻은?
   ① 사명대사   ② 신진대사

Metabolism is the chemical **processes** occurring within a living cell or organism.

> 현재분사구가
> 앞 명사를 꾸며주네요.

---

chemical **화학적인**   organism **유기체, 생물**

TEST 01 복습

▶ 단어 연결하기

archeologist	•	•	뼈
recover	•	•	조각가
bone	•	•	고고학자
tomb	•	•	복원하다, 회복하다
coffin	•	•	화학적인
excavate	•	•	신진대사
sculptor	•	•	무덤
marble	•	•	관
author	•	•	작가
metabolism	•	•	대리석
chemical	•	•	발굴하다

▶ ___ 채우기

작업해왔다 ➡ have _____

대리석으로 만들어진 ➡ _____ _____ marble.

지금까지 ➡ so _____

역대 ➡ of all _____

쓴(썼던) ➡ who _____

발생하는 ➡ _____

STEP 02

* 그 스크린은 당신의 눈에 맞추려고 빛과 영상을 **adjusts**.

→ _____ 친 단어의 뜻은?
   ① 파괴하다.   ② 조절하다.

The screen **adjusts** light and image to fit your eyes.

* 그들은 현 시점에서 한국 경제가 **unstable**하다고 결론지었다.

→ _____ 친 단어의 뜻은?
   ① 안전한   ② 불안전한

They concluded that Korea's economy is **unstable** at this point.

stable(안전한) / unstable(불안전한)

fit 맞추다, 알맞은   conclude 결론짓다

＊ 연구원들은 체육(신체적 교육)이 어린이 성장에 매우 중요한 역할을 한다고 **concluded.**

　➡　.......................... 친 단어의 뜻은?
　　① 부인했다.　　　　② 결론 내렸다.

The researchers **concluded** that physical education plays a very important role for growing children.

＊ 현재 4선 국회의원은 모든 혐의를 뻔뻔하게 **is denying.**

　➡　.......................... 친 단어의 뜻은?
　　① 인정하고 있다.　　　　　② 부인하고 있다.

> 원래 4선은 four terms(복수)이지만 여기서는 명사를 꾸며주는 형용사이므로 단수로 사용됩니다.

Presently, the four-term lawmaker **is** shamelessly **denying** all of the allegations.

play a role 역할을 하다　　　shame 수치, 부끄럽다
shameless 부끄러운 줄 모르는, 뻔뻔한　　　allegation 혐의, 의혹

＊ 펜싱 결투하는 동안 충돌하는 **swords**의 소리는 관중들에게 짜릿함을 불러일으킨다.

➡  친 단어의 뜻은?
  ① 무   ② 검

The sound of the **swords** clashing together during a fencing duel invokes a thrill in spectators.

＊ 마타하리는 1917년 독일과 프랑스 사이에서 이중간첩의 **suspicion**을 받아 처형당했다.

➡ 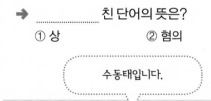 친 단어의 뜻은?
  ① 상   ② 혐의

수동태입니다.

Mata Hari was executed in 1917 under **suspicion** of being a double agent between German and France.

duel 결투, 다툼   invoke 끌어내다, 호소하다   spectator 관중, 구경꾼
execute 처형하다, 집행하다

TEST 02 복습

▶ 단어 연결하기

adjust •	• 현재
conclude •	• 부인하다
unstable •	• 조정하다
economy •	• 결론 내리다
researcher •	• 이중간첩
presently •	• 불안전한
deny •	• 경제
sword •	• 혐의, 의심
spectator •	• 관중
suspicion •	• 검
double agent •	• 연구원

▶ ___ 채우기

당신의 눈에 맞추려고 ➡ ____ _____ your eyes

현시점에서 ➡ at _____ point

체육(신체적 교육) ➡ _____ education

4선 국회의원 ➡ four- _____ lawmaker

충돌하는 ➡ _____ together

처형당했다 ➡ was _____

* 여러분은 고기를 먹는 것에 대한 <u>ethics</u>를 논의하고 있는 사자와 호랑이를 볼 수 없지 않은가?

→ .... 친 단어의 뜻은?
① 범죄   ② 윤리(문제)

> "지각(감각)동사 다음 목적어 다음 동사원형" 익숙하지요.
> 여기서 동사원형은 부정사가 못 온다는 말입니다. 그러니 상황에 따라
> 지금처럼 현재분사 또는 다른 상황에서는 과거분사도 올 수 있어요.

You don't see lions and tigers debating the **ethics** of eating meat, do you?

* 다빈치는 인체를 가능한 한 자연스럽게 그리기 위해서 **anatomy**를 공부하기 시작했다.

→ .... 친 단어의 뜻은?
① 추상화   ② 해부학

Da Vinci started his study in **anatomy** in order to paint the human body as naturally as possible.

> as … as 사이에는 형용사나 부사의 원급이 옵니다.
> 절대 비교급과 최상급은 올 수 없습니다.

in order to ~ (so as to ~) ~하기 위해서

* 교육의 효율성이 이번 **debate**에서 가장 중요한 주제이다.

➡ .... 친 단어의 뜻은?
 ① 전투　　　　　② 토론

> The effectiveness of education is the most important issue for this **debate**.

* 남아프리카 공화국은 넬슨 만델라의 얼굴이 담긴 새 지폐를 **issue** 할 예정이다.

➡ .... 친 단어의 뜻은?
 ① 판매하다.　　　② 발행하다.

> South Africa will **issue** a new bank note with the face of Nelson Mandela.

---

effectiveness 효율성　　　issue 문제, 쟁점, 발행하다　　　bank note(=bill) 지폐

＊ 게다가, 녹색은 사람들을 편하게 해주고 스트레스를 **relieves**.

➡ .... 친 단어의 뜻은?
① 증가시키다. ② 완화시키다.

In addition, green makes people feel comfortable and **relieves**
their stress.

＊ 1993년 그 부부는 이혼했고 롤링은 우울증으로 **was diagnosed**.

➡ .... 친 단어의 뜻은?
① 진정되었다. ② 진단받았다.

In 1993, the couple divorced and Rowling **was diagnosed** with
depression.

comfortable 편안한   divorce 이혼하다   depression 우울(증)

TEST 03 복습

▶ **단어 연결하기**

debate •	• 우울(증)
meat •	• 진단하다
anatomy •	• 이혼(하다)
effectiveness •	• 완화시키다
issue •	• 편안한
comfortable •	• 발행하다, 주제
relieve •	• 효율성
divorce •	• 해부학
diagnose •	• 고기
depression •	• 토론, 논의하다

▶ **___ 채우기**

논의하고 있는 ➜ _____

가능한 한 자연스럽게 ➜ as _____ as possible

가장 중요한 주제 ➜ the _____ _____ issue

게다가 ➜ in _____

21

* 소가 늘어나면서 **meadow**는 황무지로 변하고 소들은 결국 굶어 죽게 될 것이다.

➡ .... 친 단어의 뜻은?
① 해변   ② 초원

> More cows will turn the **meadow** into barren land and the cows will end up dying of hunger.

'end up ~ing'는
'결국 ~하게 되다'라는 숙어입니다.

* 방문자들은 1977년 이후로 **erosion**의 문제 때문에 스톤헨지 안으로 들어가는 것이 금지되었다.

➡ .... 친 단어의 뜻은?
① 식사   ② 부식(침식)

> Visitors have been banned from stepping inside Stonehenge since 1977, due to problems with **erosion**.

barren 메마른   ban 금지하다

* 가장 빨리 성장하고 있는 국가로서 중국은 우주탐사에서 **is progressing**.

➡ .... 친 단어의 뜻은?
　① 퇴보하고 있다.　　　② 진보하고 있다.

As the fastest growing nation, China **is progressing** in space exploration.

* 미국은 북한의 핵무기 계획을 다시 한 번 **denounced**.

➡ .... 친 단어의 뜻은?
　① 옹호했다.　　② 비난했다.

The United States once again **denounced** North Korea for its nuclear weapons plan.

exploration 탐험, 탐사　　　nuclear 원자력, 핵의

* 최근 한국 화장품 회사들은 동물실험을 종료할 것이라고 **announced**.

➡ .... 친 단어의 뜻은?

　① 비난했다.　　　② 발표했다.

Recently, Korean cosmetic companies **announced** they will stop animal testing.

* 티벳에서 온 그 현자는 인류의 운명에 대한 **prophetic** 말들을 했다.

➡ .... 친 단어의 뜻은?

　① 멍청한　　　② 예언적인

The wise man from Tibet gave **prophetic** words about the destiny of humankind.

cosmetic 화장품　　　destiny 운명

TEST 04 복습

▶ 단어 연결하기

cow •	• 소
meadow •	• 메마른
barren •	• 침식, 부식
ban •	• 탐험, 탐사
erosion •	• 핵무기의
progress •	• 예언적인
exploration •	• 운명
denounce •	• 발표하다
nuclear •	• 비난하다
announce •	• 진보하다
prophetic •	• 금지하다
destiny •	• 초원

▶ ___ 채우기

결국 굶어 죽게 될 것이다 ➡ will end ___ dying of _____

문제 때문에 ➡ due ___ problems

가장 빨리 성장하고 있는 국가로서 ➡ ___ the _____ growing nation

티벳에서 온 ➡ _____ Tibet

* 많은 일본 시민들과 지역 **residents**는 오래된 원자로에 대해 걱정해 왔다.

➜ .... 친 단어의 뜻은?
① 일베들   ② 주민들

Many Japanese citizens and local **residents** have been concerned about the aging reactors.

* 세계 최초의 대학이 기원전 700년에 인도에서 **was established**.

➜ .... 친 단어의 뜻은?
① 걸어다녔다.   ② 설립되었다.

The first university in the world **was established** in India in 700 BC.

age 나이, 나이를 먹다, 오래되다   reactor 원자로, 반응장치

* 공룡의 멸종에 대한 많은 **assumptions**가 있다.

➡ .... 친 단어의 뜻은?
  ① 요청   ② 가설

There are many **assumptions** about their extinction.

* **Local** 여행사들도 전통시장이라는 주제를 가진 여행 상품들을 출시할 계획이다.

➡ .... 친 단어의 뜻은?
  ① 해외(의)   ② 지역(의)

Local tour agencies also plan to release tour products themed with traditional markets.

과거분사구가 명사를 후치수식합니다.

extinction 멸종, 소멸   release 출시하다, 방출하다   theme 주제
themed 주제를 가진, 테마가 있는

* 현재의 미국 교육 시스템은 지방 정부의 세금 **revenue**에 의존하고 있다.

➡ .... 친 단어의 뜻은?
①　수출　　　　　②　수입, 수익

The present American education system relies on local governments' tax **revenue**.

* 직독직해 공식적 자료는 보여준다. / 총 수출량이 2.7%까지 작년에 감소했음을 / 수입이 12%까지 **surged**한 반면에

➡ .... 친 단어의 뜻은?
①　급감했다.　　　②　급등했다.

Official data has revealed / that total exports shrank by 2.7 percent last year / while imports **surged** by 12 percent.

rely on 의존하다　　shrink 감소하다　　export 수출(하다)　　import 수입(하다)

28

TEST 05 복습

▶ 단어 연결하기

resident	• •	세금
assumption	• •	상품, 제품
extinction	• •	지역의
local	• •	수출(하다)
release	• •	소멸, 멸종
product	• •	가설, 가정
rely on	• •	주민
tax	• •	출시하다, 방출하다
revenue	• •	급등하다
export	• •	감소하다, 움츠리다
shrink	• •	수입, 수익
surge	• •	~에 의존하다
establish	• •	설립하다, 확립하다

▶ ___ 채우기

~에 대해 걱정해 왔다 ➡ have been _____ about

전통시장이라는 주제를 가진 ➡ _____ with traditional market

12%까지 ➡ ____ 12 percent

STEP 01

+ Archeologists have worked to recover the bones for the past five months.

+ In his tomb, there is a big coffin made of marble.

+ Archeologists have excavated over 500 tombs at the site so far.

+ He was a great sculptor and his marble statue, "David" is one of the most famous sculptures of all time.

+ She is a world-famous author who wrote the Harry Potter series.

+ Metabolism is the chemical processes occurring within a living cell or organism.

STEP 02

+ The screen adjusts light and image to fit your eyes.

+ They concluded that Korea's economy is unstable at this point.

+ The researchers concluded that physical education plays a very important role for growing children.

+ Presently, the four-term lawmaker is shamelessly denying all of the allegations.

+ The sound of the swords clashing together during a fencing duel invokes a thrill in spectators.

+ Mata Hari was executed in 1917 under suspicion of being a double agent between German and France.

STEP 03

+ You don't see lions and tigers debating the ethics of eating meat, do you?

+ Da Vinci started his study in anatomy in order to paint the human body as naturally as possible.

+ The effectiveness of education is the most important issue for this debate.

+ South Africa will issue a new bank note with the face of Nelson Mandela.

- In addition, green makes people feel comfortable and relieves their stress.
- In 1993, the couple divorced and Rowling was diagnosed with depression.

STEP 04

- More cows will turn the meadow into barren land and the cows will end up dying of hunger.
- Visitors have been banned from stepping inside Stonehenge since 1977, due to problems with erosion.
- As the fastest growing nation, China is progressing in space exploration.
- The United States once again denounced North Korea for its nuclear weapons plan.
- Recently, Korean cosmetic companies announced they will stop animal testing.
- The wise man from Tibet gave prophetic words about the destiny of humankind.

STEP 05

- Many Japanese citizens and local residents have been concerned about the aging reactors.
- The first university in the world was established in India in 700 BC.
- There are many assumptions about their extinction.
- Local tour agencies also plan to release tour products themed with traditional markets.
- The present American education system relies on local governments' tax revenue.
- Official data has revealed that total exports shrank by 2.7 percent last year while imports surged by 12 percent.

* 또래 **mediation** 프로그램이 학생들 사이에서 학교 폭력 감소에 기여하고 있다.

➡ .... 친 단어의 뜻은?
   ① 분노   ② 중재

> The peer **mediation** program has contributed to a drop in school violence among students.

* 하지만 양측은 평양이 핵 **negotiations**에 돌아왔을 때 식량지원을 승인했다.

➡ .... 친 단어의 뜻은?
   ① 폭발   ② 협상

> But both approved food aid when Pyongyang returned to nuclear **negotiations**.

peer 또래, 동료   contribute 기여하다, 공헌하다   violence 폭력
approve 승인하다   aid 지원, 원조

＊ 지속적인 피로는 정신적 <u>clarity</u>의 부족을 야기할 수 있다.

➡ .... 친 단어의 뜻은?
　① 모호성　　　　② 명료성

Persistent fatigue can cause a lack of mental **clarity**.

＊ 그 **vague** 소문은 거짓으로 드러났다. 그럼에도 불구하고 약간의 의심이 사라지지 않았다.

➡ .... 친 단어의 뜻은?
　① 맛있는　　　　② 모호한, 애매한

The **vague** rumor proved to be false. Nevertheless, some doubt didn't disappear.

persistent 지속적인, 끊임없는　　fatigue 피로　　lack 부족, 결핍
prove 드러나다, 증명하다

* 건강을 **maintaining** 고등학교 3학년 학생이 직면하는 가장 큰 도전과제 중 하나이다.

➜ .... 친 단어의 뜻은?
  ① 이해하는 것은   ② 유지하는 것은

Maintaining good health is one of the biggest challenges facing high school seniors.

현재분사구가 명사를 후치수식합니다.

* 최근 애플은 자사의 태블릿 PC를 기부함으로써 사회에 **to contribute** 결심했다.

➜ .... 친 단어의 뜻은?
  ① 수익을 창출하기로   ② 기여하기로, 공헌하기로

Recently, Apple decided **to contribute** to society by donating its tablet PCs.

<by ~ing>는 "~함으로써" 숙어입니다.

---

senior 연장자, 선배, 최상급생   donate 기부하다

TEST 06 복습

▶ 단어 연결하기

peer •		• 피로
mediation •		• 협상
violence •		• 지원(하다)
approve •		• 승인하다
aid •		• 폭력
negotiation •		• 중재
fatigue •		• 동료
clarity •		• 명료(성)
vague •		• 모호한, 애매한
prove •		• 드러나다, ~임이 판명되다
maintain •		• 유지하다
contribute •		• 기부하다
donate •		• 기여하다, 공헌하다

▶ ___ 채우기

학생들 사이에서 → _____ students

야기할 수 있다 → can _____

그럼에도 불구하고 → _____

고등학교 3학년 학생이 직면하는 → _____ high school _____

기부함으로써 → ____ donating

* **Prudent** 투자자는 매입할 주식을 선택하는 데 주의하고 인내한다.

→ _____ 친 단어의 뜻은?
① 손 큰   ② 신중한

> imprudent (신중하지 못한, 경솔한)

The **prudent** investor is careful and patient in choosing stocks for purchase.

* 그에 따르면 시를 쓰는 것은 그를 **modest**하고 정직하고 온건하게 유지하도록 돕는다.

→ _____ 친 단어의 뜻은?
① 근엄한   ② 겸손한

According to him, writing poems helps him stay **modest**, honest and moderate.

---

invest 투자하다   investor 투자자   stock 주식, 재고
purchase 구입(하다)   moderate 온건한, 적당한

* 환자는 **patient**해야 한다.

➡ .... 친 단어의 뜻은?
① 슬퍼하는　　② 인내하는

A patient has to be **patient.**

* 새로운 연구에 따르면 인터넷에 중독된 십대들은 **moderate** 인터넷 사용
자들보다 아이큐가 더 낮다고 합니다.

➡ .... 친 단어의 뜻은?
① 열성적인　　② 적절한

관계대명사 who절이
앞 명사를 수식합니다.

According to a new study, teenagers who are addicted to the
Internet have lower IQs than **moderate** Internet users.

patient 환자, 인내하는　　　addict 중독시키다, 중독자

* 그녀의 **mind** 따위는 신경쓰지마.

➡ .... 친 단어의 뜻은?
  ① 몸매　　　　② 마음

Never mind about her **mind.**

> mind가 동사일 때는
> "~ 신경쓰다, ~ 꺼리다"라는 뜻이 있습니다.

* **Ferry** 세월호 재난(참사)은 사람들의 마음속에 깊은 상처를 남겼다.

➡ .... 친 단어의 뜻은?
  ① 잠수함　　　　② 여객선

The **ferry** Sewol disaster has left a deep scar in people's mind.

mind 마음, 꺼리다, 신경쓰다　　　disaster 재난　　　scar 상처

TEST 07 복습

▶ **단어 연결하기**

prudent •		• 신중한
investor •		• 투자자
stock •		• 주식
purchase •		• 매입(하다), 구입하다
modest •		• 겸손한
honest •		• 정직한
patient •		• 인내하는, 환자
moderate •		• 적절한, 온건한
mind •		• 마음, 신경쓰다, 꺼리다
ferry •		• 여객선
disaster •		• 재난
scar •		• 상처

▶ **___ 채우기**

선택하는 데 ➡ ___ choosing

그에 따르면 ➡ _____ ___ him

중독된 십대들 ➡ teenagers _____ are _____

39

* 미량의 방사능 물질이라도 그것들이 장기적으로 **are accumulated** 되면
  인체에 해로울 수 있다.

  ➡ .... 친 단어의 뜻은?
  ① 분산되다.   ② 축적되다.

  Even the slightest amount of radioactive materials can be
  harmful to humans, if they **are accumulated** in the body over
  the long term.

* 미국 전역의 연구원과 과학자들은 왜 이렇게 많은 벌 집단들이 죽고 있는지
  를 **to figure out** 애써 왔습니다.

  ➡ .... 친 단어의 뜻은?
  ① 무시하려고   ② 이해하려고, 파악하려고

  Researchers and scientists all over the U.S. have been trying **to
  figure out** why so many bee colonies are dying.

radioactive 방사능   harmful 해로운   accumulate 축척하다
figure out 이해하다, 파악하다   colony 집단, 식민지

* 일부 상황에서 불합리한 주장을 **ignoring**은 좋은 전략이다.

➡ .... 친 단어의 뜻은?
  ① 부화뇌동하는 것   ② 무시하는 것

In some cases, **ignoring** unreasonable arguments is a good strategy.

* 그녀는 자신의 계획을 개선하기 위해 어떠한 **constructive** 비판이라도 환영했다.

➡ .... 친 단어의 뜻은?
  ① 급한   ② 건설적인

She welcomed any **constructive** criticism to improve her plan.

argument 주장, 논쟁   strategy 전략   criticism 비판   improve 개선하다

41

＊ 하지만 무엇보다 우리 모두는 보행자가 차보다 **priority** 해야 한다는 것을 진실로 알아야 한다.

→ .... 친 단어의 뜻은?
  ① 건강   ② 우선(권)

<be aware of 명사, be aware that 주어+동사…>이고 의미는 "…를 알다"입니다. 자주 사용됩니다.

First of all, however, we all have to be truly aware that walkers should be given **priority** over cars.

＊ 그것들은 단지 나에게 위험하고 작고 **annoying** 동물들이었다.

→ .... 친 단어의 뜻은?
  ① 안전한   ② 짜증나는

They were nothing but dangerous, tiny and **annoying** animals to me.

nothing but에서 but은 '~을 제외하고'라는 의미입니다. 그래서 그 의미를 합치면 '~을 제외하고 아무것도 아니다' 즉 '단지'라는 의미입니다.

aware 알고 있는, 인식하는   annoy 짜증나다, 괴롭히다

TEST 08 복습

▶ 단어 연결하기

radioactive •	• 해로운
harmful •	• 불합리한
accumulate •	• 짜증나게 하다
figure out •	• 우선(권)
bee •	• 방사능의
ignore •	• 전략
unreasonable •	• 비판
strategy •	• 축적하다
constructive •	• 파악하다, 이해하다
criticism •	• 건설적인
priority •	• 무시하다
annoy •	• 벌

▶ ___ 채우기

장기적으로 ➡ over the long _____

그녀의 계획을 개선하기 위해 ➡ ____ improve her _____

진실로 알아야 한다 ➡ have to ____ truly _____

단지 ➡ nothing _____

* 귀하의 관심에 감사드리며 차후 **reference**하도록 귀하의 정보를 파일에 보관하고 있겠습니다.

➜ _____ 친 단어의 뜻은?
① 감독　　　　　② 참고

We appreciate your interest and will keep your information on file for future **reference**.

* 그것이 **innovation**보다는 오히려 표준이 되면서 사람들은 그것을 보는 데 익숙해질 것이다.

➜ _____ 친 단어의 뜻은?
① 혁명　　　　　② 혁신

As it becomes the norm rather than an **innovation**, people will be used to seeing it.

be used to ~ing: ~에 익숙하다. / be used to ~: ~에 사용되다.
모양이 비슷합니다. 확실히 암기합시다.

appreciate 감사하다, 감상하다, 이해하다　　　norm 표준

* 이러한 모든 요소들이 영국에서 산업 **Revolution**이 시작되는 데 필요한 환경을 조성하였다.

➡ .... 친 단어의 뜻은?
① 구성　　　　② 혁명

All of these factors created the necessary environment for the Industrial **Revolution** to begin in Great Britain.

* 그 시리즈는 73개의 언어로 번역되었다. 그리고 독자들은 그 책의 흥미로운 이야기를 **appreciated**.

➡ .... 친 단어의 뜻은?
① 감시했다.　　② 감상했다.

The series was translated into 73 languages and readers **appreciated** the books' interesting stories.

factor 요소　　translate 번역하다　　appreciate 감상하다, 감사하다, 이해하다

* 의사는 제이크에게 두통을 **to lessen** 도움이 되는 처방전을 써주었다.

➡ .... 친 단어의 뜻은?

① 연장시키는 데   ② 완화하는 데

> The doctor wrote Jake a prescription to help **to lessen** his headaches.

* 사람이 언어 폭력을 당하면(말로 학대받으면) **resentment**와 우울함을 느끼기 쉽다.

➡ .... 친 단어의 뜻은?

① 평정심   ② 분노

> If someone is verbally abused, they are likely to feel **resentment** and depression.

prescription 처방전   lessen 완화하다, 줄이다   verbally 말로, 언어로
abuse 학대하다, 남용하다

46

TEST 09 복습

▶ 단어 연결하기

reference •	• 분노
norm •	• 참고
innovation •	• 요소
factor •	• 표준
revolution •	• 학대하다, 남용하다
appreciate •	• 혁명
prescription •	• 혁신
lessen •	• 감사하다, 감상하다
headache •	• 언어적으로
verbally •	• 두통
abuse •	• 완화하다, 줄이다
resentment •	• 처방(전)

▶ ___ 채우기

그것을 보는 데 익숙해질 것이다 → will be _____ to _____ it

번역되었다 → was _____

느끼기 쉽다 → are _____ to _____

* 사회적 **deviance**와 범죄에 대한 연구.

➡ .... 친 단어의 뜻은?
① 해탈   ② 일탈

A study of social **deviance** and crime.

* 옹호자들은 동물 **experiments**가 몇몇 동물을 희생하여 수백만의 삶에 도움을 줄 수 있다고 믿는다.

➡ .... 친 단어의 뜻은?
① 보호   ② 실험

Supporters believe animal **experiments** can help the lives of millions of people at the cost of a few animals.

crime 범죄   at the cost of ~을 희생하여

* 그 아이는 유전적 문제 때문에 **deformed**로 태어났다.

➜ ·················· 친 단어의 뜻은?
① 정상인　　　　② 불구의

The child was born **deformed** because of a genetic problem.

* 허리케인의 **intensity**와 빈도는 증가하지 않았다.

➜ ·················· 친 단어의 뜻은?
① 피해　　　　② 강도

Neither the **intensity** nor the frequency of hurricanes has increased.

neither A nor B: A, B 둘 다 아니다.

deform 변형시키다, 기형으로 만들다　　genetic 유전적　　frequency 빈도

49

* 유명인들은 대중 앞에서 그들의 정체를 **to conceal** 때때로 외모를 바꾼다.

➡ .... 친 단어의 뜻은?
  ① 과시하기 위해   ② 숨기기 위해

Celebrities sometimes change their looks **to conceal** their identity in public.

* 많은 현대 사회에서 부자들은 자신들의 부를 **to show off**(=boast) 비싼 명품 옷을 입는다.

➡ .... 친 단어의 뜻은?
  ① 숨기기 위해   ② 과시하기 위해

<the+형용사>는 "~한 사람들"로 자주 해석됩니다.

In many current societies, the rich wear expensive designer clothes **to show off** their wealth.

celebrity 유명인사   identity 정체, 신원   current 현재의, 흐름
wealth 재산, 부

50

TEST 10 복습

▶ 단어 연결하기

deviance •	• 유명인
crime •	• 불구인
experiment •	• 과시하다, 자랑하다
deformed •	• 일탈
genetic •	• 범죄
intensity •	• 빈도
frequency •	• 부, 재산
celebrity •	• 실험
conceal •	• 유전적인
identity •	• 강도
show off •	• 숨기다
wealth •	• 정체(성)

▶ ___ 채우기

몇몇 동물들을 희생하여 → at the _____ of a few animals

A, B 둘 다 아니다 → _____ A nor B

대중 앞에서 → in _____

부자들 → _____ rich

51

STEP 06

+ The peer mediation program has contributed to a drop in school violence among students.
+ But both approved food aid when Pyongyang returned to nuclear negotiations.
+ Persistent fatigue can cause a lack of mental clarity.
+ The vague rumor proved to be false. Nevertheless, some doubt didn't disappear.
+ Maintaining good health is one of the biggest challenges facing high school seniors.
+ Recently, Apple decided to contribute to society by donating its tablet PCs.

STEP 07

+ The prudent investor is careful and patient in choosing stocks for purchase.
+ According to him, writing poems helps him stay modest, honest and moderate.
+ A patient has to be patient.
+ According to a new study, teenagers who are addicted to the Internet have lower IQs than moderate Internet users.
+ Never mind about her mind.
+ The ferry Sewol disaster has left a deep scar in people's mind.

STEP 08

+ Even the slightest amount of radioactive materials can be harmful to humans, if they are accumulated in the body over the long term.
+ Researchers and scientists all over the U.S. have been trying to figure out why so many bee colonies are dying.
+ In some cases, ignoring unreasonable arguments is a good strategy.
+ She welcomed any constructive criticism to improve her plan.

+ First of all, however, we all have to be truly aware that walkers should be given priority over cars.
+ They were nothing but dangerous, tiny and annoying animals to me.

STEP 09

+ We appreciate your interest and will keep your information on file for future reference.
+ As it becomes the norm rather than an innovation, people will be used to seeing it.
+ All of these factors created the necessary environment for the Industrial Revolution to begin in Great Britain.
+ The series was translated into 73 languages and readers appreciated the books' interesting stories.
+ The doctor wrote Jake a prescription to help to lessen his headaches.
+ If someone is verbally abused, they are likely to feel resentment and depression.

STEP 10

+ A study of social deviance and crime.
+ Supporters believe animal experiments can help the lives of millions of people at the cost of a few animals.
+ The child was born deformed because of a genetic problem.
+ Neither the intensity nor the frequency of hurricanes has increased.
+ Celebrities sometimes change their looks to conceal their identity in public.
+ In many current societies, the rich wear expensive designer clothes to show off their wealth.

STEP 11

* 대부분의 사람들이 보는 푸른 하늘은 **사실 공기가 햇빛을 방해해서 생긴** **illusion**이다.

➡ .... 친 단어의 뜻은?
   ① 명상   ② 착시(현상), 착각

The blue sky that most people see is actually an **illusion** due to the interference of the sunlight with the air.

* 스웨덴에 있는 발전소들은 쓰레기를 에너지로 **can convert**.

➡ .... 친 단어의 뜻은?
   ① 전송할 수 있다.   ② 전환할 수 있다.

Power plants in Sweden **can convert** waste into energy

interference 방해   convert 전환하다   waste 쓰레기, 낭비하다

* 대부분의 국제공항은 엄청난 규모의 잔디밭이 있는데 풀과 **weeds**를 자르기 위해 많은 시간과 돈을 씁니다.

➡ .... 친 단어의 뜻은?
① 철사　　　　　② 잡초

Most International airports have huge lawns and they spend a lot of time and money to cut the grass and **weeds.**

* 국세청은 세금 탈루를 **to weed out** 116개 대기업에 대한 대대적인 세금조사에 착수했다.

➡ .... 친 단어의 뜻은?
① 보존하기 위해　　　　② 제거하기 위해

The National Tax Service launched an extensive tax probe into 116 large—size companies **to weed out** tax evaders.

lawn 잔디　　launch 착수하다, 발사하다　　extensive 대대적인, 광범위한
probe 조사(하다)　　weed out 제거하다

55

* 설탕이 많이 함유된 음료수는 비만 **diabetes** 그리고 고혈압을 유발할 수 있다.

➡ .... 친 단어의 뜻은?
① 요실금　　　　　② 당뇨

High sugar drinks may cause obesity, **diabetes** and high blood pressure.

* 인종차별주의는 역사에서 많은 끔찍한 것들에 대해 책임이 있어 왔고 현대 사회에서 항상 **should be rejected**.

➡ .... 친 단어의 뜻은?
① 인정되어야 한다.　　　② 거부되어야 한다.

Racism has been responsible for many horrible things in history and **should** always **be rejected** in modern society.

obesity 비만　　　racism 인종차별(주의)

TEST 11 복습

▶ 단어 연결하기

illusion •	• 전환하다
interference •	• 비만
convert •	• 거절하다
waste •	• 당뇨
lawn •	• 잡초, 제거하다
weed •	• 방해
tax •	• 착시, 환각
extensive •	• 책임있는
probe •	• 세금
obesity •	• 쓰레기, 낭비하다
diabetes •	• 잔디
racism •	• 인종주의
responsible •	• 조사, 탐사(하다)
reject •	• 대대적인, 광범위한

▶ ___ 채우기

대부분의 사람들이 보는 푸른 하늘

→ the blue sky _____ most people _____

많은 시간과 돈 → a _____ of time and money

고혈압 → high blood _____

* 농구에서 금속으로 된 고리 즉 **rim** 지름이 45.7센티미터이다.

➜ .... 친 단어의 뜻은?

① 공   ② 테두리

In basketball, the metal hoop, or **rim**, measures 45.7 centimeters in diameter.

> 흐름상 여기서 or은 '즉'이라는 의미입니다.

* 거친 파도와 차가운 온도 외에도 그는 또한 짙은 **fog**에 대처해야 했다.

➜ .... 친 단어의 뜻은?

① 개   ② 안개

Besides rough waves and the freezing temperature, he also had to cope with a thick **fog**.

---

measure 측정하다   diameter 지름   freeze 얼다
freezing 차가운, 몹시 추운

* 폭우로 46개 노선의 배편이 막혔으며 96척의 선박이 부두 가까이로 <u>anchor</u> 해야 했다.

  ➡   .... 친 단어의 뜻은?

     ① 숙박하다.   ② 정박하다.

> The heavy rains closed 46 shipping routes and 96 ships were forced to **anchor** near the ports.

* 파리는 그 전 해에 연합군에 의해 독일 <u>occupation</u>으로부터 해방되었다.

  ➡   .... 친 단어의 뜻은?

     ① 기업   ② 점령

> Paris was liberated by the Allied Forces from German **occupation** the previous year.

---

be forced to ~해야 하다   liberate 해방하다   ally 연합하다, 동맹국
allied 연합된   previous 이전의

* 돈은 악의 **underlying** 원인이라고들 한다.

➡ ···················· 친 단어의 뜻은?
　① 소극적인　　　② 근본적인

It is said that money is the **underlying** cause of evil.

* 여러분도 이미 아시겠지만 저는 새로운 사람들과 이야기하는 것을 그다지
  좋아하지 않는(열중하지 않는) 수줍음 많고 **passive** 여학생이었습니다.

➡ ···················· 친 단어의 뜻은?
　① 소중한　　　② 소극적인

> used to는 여기서 과거의 상태를 의미합니다(~였다).
> '그러나 현재는 아니다'라는 의미가 포함되어 있습니다.

As you may already know, I used to be a shy and **passive** girl,
not keen on talking to new people.

evil 악, 사악한　　keen 열중하는

60

TEST 12 복습

▶ 단어 연결하기

metal	지름
hoop	금속의
rim	열중한, 예민한
measure	안개
diameter	고리
fog	소극적인, 수동적인
anchor	점령
liberate	해방시키다
occupation	테두리
previous	측정하다
underlying	정박하다
evil	수줍은
shy	악
passive	근본적인
keen	이전의

▶ ___ 채우기

~에 대처해야 했다 → had to _____ with

정박해야 했다 → were _____ to anchor

연합군에 의해 → ___ the _____ Forces

61

* 대조적으로 배심원들은 애플이 자신의 **patent**를 침해했다는 삼성의 주장을 받아들이지 않았다.

→ .... 친 단어의 뜻은?
  ① 진정성　　　　② 특허

> In contrast the jurors did not accept Samsung's claim that Apple violated its **patent.**

* 비록 많은 유명한 암호해독가들이 시도해 봤지만, 아무도 그 책을 **decode** 할 수 없었다.

→ .... 친 단어의 뜻은?
  ① 대여하다.　　　② 해독하다.

> No one is able to **decode** the book although many famous code—breakers have tried.

---

juror 배심원　　　violate 침해하다

* **Population**의 관점에서 다시 통일이 되면 우리는 세계에서 17번째 인구가 많은 나라가 된다.

➡ .... 친 단어의 뜻은?
   ① 면적   ② 인구

In terms of **population**, we will be the world's 17th populous country if reunified.

> if 다음에 주어(we)와 be동사(are)가 생략되었다.
> 흐름상 알 수 있습니다.

* 상사는 필요한 모든 물품을 구입하기 위해서 비서에게 <u>errand</u>를 보냈다.

➡ .... 친 단어의 뜻은?
   ① 약국   ② 심부름

The boss sent the secretary on an <u>errand</u> to buy all the necessary supplies.

---

populous 인구가 많은   reunify 다시 통일하다   secretary 비서
supply 물품, 공급하다

* 하지만 많은 **pharmacies**는 약을 가게에서 파는 것이 위험한 일이라고 말한다.

➡ .... 친 단어의 뜻은?
  ① 병원들　　　　② 약국들

But many **pharmacies** say that it is dangerous to sell drugs at stores.

* 서울 버스 7천 5백여 대가 파업에 참가했다. 그리고 5백만 명의 **passengers**에게 영향을 미쳤다.

➡ .... 친 단어의 뜻은?
  ① 시민　　　　② 승객

Some 7,500 buses in Seoul took part in the protest and affected 5 million **passengers**.

drug 약, 마약　　　take part in 참가하다　　　affect 영향을 미치다

TEST 13 복습

▶ 단어 연결하기

juror •		• 배심원
claim •		• 주장(하다)
violate •		• 침해하다, 위반하다
patent •		• 특허
decode •		• 해독하다
population •		• 인구
secretary •		• 비서
errand •		• 심부름
pharmacy •		• 약국
affect •		• 영향을 미치다
passenger •		• 승객

▶ ___ 채우기

대조적으로 → in _____

인구의 관점에서 → in _____ of population

파업에 참가했다 → took _____ in the protest

* **Camels**는 물을 마시지 않고 사막에서 여러 날 살 수 있는 동물입니다.

➡ .... 친 단어의 뜻은?
   ① 하마   ② 낙타

Camels are animals that can survive for many days in the desert without drinking water.

* 여러분이 기독교인이든 아니든, 여러분은 아마도 예수를 배반했던 **disciple**, 유다의 이야기에 익숙하다.

➡ .... 친 단어의 뜻은?
   ① 정치인   ② 제자

Whether you are Christian or not, you are probably familiar with the story of Judas, the **disciple** who betrayed Jesus.

survive 생존하다   familiar 익숙한, 친근한   betray 배반하다

* **Sweat**는 당신을 결코 배신하지 않는다.

➡ .... 친 단어의 뜻은?
  ① 콧물　　　　　② 땀

Sweat never betrays you.

* **Pollen**은 바람에 의해 퍼지고 씨앗을 수정시킵니다.

➡ .... 친 단어의 뜻은?
  ① 밀가루　　　　② 꽃가루

The **pollen** is spread by the wind and fertilizes the seeds.

spread – spread – spread 퍼지다　　fertilize 수정시키다, 비옥하게 하다

* 성형수술은 겉모습이 전부라고 생각하는 **shallow** 그리고 편협한 생각을 지닌 사람들을 위한 거야.

→ .... 친 단어의 뜻은?
　　① 신중한　　　　　② 얄팍한

Plastic surgery is for **shallow** and closed—minded people who think that looks are everything.

* 직독직해 그러므로 **street stalls**가 허용되어야 한다. / 그들이 소비자와 판매자들을 돕기 때문에 / 그리고 그들 둘 다는 보통 저소득 계층 출신이다.

→ .... 친 단어의 뜻은?
　　① 대형 체인점　　　　　② 노점상

Therefore, **street stalls** should be permitted / because they help consumers and sellers, / both of whom usually come from low income levels.

> , who는 대체로 '그리고 그(녀)는'으로 해석된다. 그래서
> , both of whom은 '그리고 그들 둘 다는'으로 해석합시다.

surgery 수술, 외과　　　stall 칸막이, 진열대　　　income 소득

TEST 14 복습

▶ 단어 연결하기

camel	•	•	퍼뜨리다
survive	•	•	익숙한, 친숙한
desert	•	•	소득
familiar	•	•	수정시키다
disciple	•	•	성형수술
betray	•	•	배반하다
sweat	•	•	소비자
pollen	•	•	노점상
spread	•	•	얄팍한
fertilize	•	•	생존하다
seed	•	•	사막
plastic surgery	•	•	제자
shallow	•	•	땀
street stall	•	•	꽃가루
consumer	•	•	씨
income	•	•	낙타

▶ ___ 채우기

물을 마시지 않고 → _____ drinking water
바람에 의해 퍼지다 → is _____ ____ the wind
허용되어야 한다 → should _____ permitted

* 아르헨티나는 많은 양의 꿀, 콩, 해바라기 씨, 옥수수 그리고 **wheat**를 생산한다.

→ .... 친 단어의 뜻은?
  ① 축구공   ② 밀

Argentina produces a lot of honey, soybeans, sunflower seeds, corn and **wheat**.

* 직독직해 많은 미국인들은 이민자들과 **illegal** 이민자들을 경계한다. / 그들이 일자리와 사회적 편익을 뺏어갈까봐 두려워하면서

→ .... 친 단어의 뜻은?
  ① 합법적인   ② 불법적인

Many Americans are wary of immigrants and **illegal** immigrants / fearing that they would take away jobs and social benefits.

be wary of 경계하다   take away 제거하다   benefit 이익

＊ 하이에나는 그들의 **prey**의 피부, 이빨, 뿔 그리고 뼈까지도 먹고 소화시킬 수 있다.

➡ .... 친 단어의 뜻은?
    ① 포식자   ② 먹이

Hyenas can eat and digest their **prey** with its skin, teeth, horns and bones.

＊ **Acid** 비를 경계해라(주의해라).

➡ .... 친 단어의 뜻은?
    ① 봄   ② 산성(의)

Be wary of **acid** rain.

horn **뿔, 경적**

* 작은 아기 거북이들은 부화하자마자 종종 **predators**에게 희생되고 맙니다.

➡ .... 친 단어의 뜻은?
  ① 상어들   ② 포식자들

Small baby turtles often fall victim to **predators** right after hatching.

* 하지만, 물린 데 **scratch** 마세요!

➡ .... 친 단어의 뜻은?
  ① 물다   ② 긁다

However, don't **scratch** the area where you were bitten !

hatch 부화하다   bite – bit – bitten 물다

TEST 15 복습

▶ **단어 연결하기**

produce •	• 생산하다
soybean •	• 먹이
wheat •	• 긁다, 할퀴다
immigrant •	• 불법적인
illegal •	• 콩
fear •	• 뿔
benefit •	• 산성의
digest •	• 밀
prey •	• 이민자
horn •	• 두려워하다
acid •	• 거북이
turtle •	• 소화하다
predator •	• 이익
scratch •	• 포식자

▶ ___ **채우기**

뺏어갈거다 ➡ would take _____
~를 경계하다 ➡ be _____ of
부화하자마자 ➡ _____ after hatching
물린 데 ➡ the area where you were _____

STEP 11

+ The blue sky that most people see is actually an illusion due to the interference of the sunlight with the air.

+ Power plants in Sweden can convert waste into energy.

+ Most International airports have huge lawns and they spend a lot of time and money to cut the grass and weeds.

+ The National Tax Service launched an extensive tax probe into 116 large-size companies to weed out tax evaders.

+ High sugar drinks may cause obesity, diabetes and high blood pressure.

+ Racism has been responsible for many horrible things in history and should always be rejected in modern society.

STEP 12

+ In basketball, the metal hoop, or rim, measures 45.7 centimeters in diameter.

+ Besides rough waves and the freezing temperature, he also had to cope with a thick fog.

+ The heavy rains closed 46 shipping routes and 96 ships were forced to anchor near the ports.

+ Paris was liberated by the Allied Forces from German occupation the previous year.

+ It is said that money is the underlying cause of evil.

+ As you may already know, I used to be a shy and passive girl, not keen on talking to new people.

+ ## STEP 13

+ In contrast the jurors did not accept Samsung's claim that Apple violated its patent.

+ No one is able to decode the book although many famous code-breakers have tried.

+ In terms of population, we will be the world's 17th populous country if reunified.

+ The boss sent the secretary on an errand to buy all the necessary supplies.

+ But many pharmacies say that it is dangerous to sell drugs at stores.

+ Some 7,500 buses in Seoul took part in the protest and affected 5 million passengers.

STEP 14

+ Camels are animals that can survive for many days in the desert without drinking water.

+ Whether you are Christian or not, you are probably familiar with the story of Judas, the disciple who betrayed Jesus.

+ Sweat never betrays you.

+ The pollen is spread by the wind and fertilizes the seeds.

+ Plastic surgery is for shallow and closed-minded people who think that looks are everything.

+ Therefore, street stalls should be permitted because they help consumers and sellers, both of whom usually come from low income levels.

STEP 15

+ Argentina produces a lot of honey, soybeans, sunflower seeds, corn and wheat.

+ Many Americans are wary of immigrants and illegal immigrants fearing that they would take away jobs and social benefits.

+ Hyenas can eat and digest their prey with its skin, teeth, horns and bones.

+ Be wary of acid rain.

+ Small baby turtles often fall victim to predators right after hatching.

+ However, don't scratch the area where you were bitten!

* 배는 **horizon** 저편으로 사라져 갔다.

➡ .... 친 단어의 뜻은?
   ① 수직선   ② 수평선

The ship faded away below the **horizon**.

* 한국과 호주는 현재 **diplomatic** 관계를 맺은 지 50주년을 축하하고 있다.

➡ .... 친 단어의 뜻은?
   ① 연인   ② 외교(의)

Korea and Australia are currently celebrating their 50th anniversary of **diplomatic** relations.

celebrate 축하하다   relation 관계

* 그의 행동은 소수의 사람들에 의해 **has been applauded**. 그러나 많은 다른 사람들에 의해 비난받았다.

➡ .... 친 단어의 뜻은?
 ① 경멸받았다. ② 찬사받았다.

His action **has been applauded** by a few but criticized by many others.

* 존경하는 것의 반대말은 **to despise**와 미워하는 것이다.

➡ .... 친 단어의 뜻은?
 ① 부러워하는 것 ② 경멸하는 것

The opposite words of respect are **to despise** and hate.

applaud 박수치다, 칭찬하다   criticize 비난하다   opposite 반대의, 반의어

* 전 세계의 재정 **analysts**는 현재 원-달러 환율이 당분간 계속될 것이라고 예측한다.

➡ .... 친 단어의 뜻은?
　① 사채업자　　　② 분석가

Financial **analysts** across the world predict the current won-dollar exchange rate to continue for the time being.

* 그 회사는 의료 보험, **pensions**, 직원 할인과 같은 혜택을 제공한다.

➡ .... 친 단어의 뜻은?
　① 야식　　　② 연금

The company offers benefits such as health insurance, **pensions** and employee discounts.

predict 예측하다　　rate 비율

TEST 16 복습

▶ 단어 연결하기

horizon	연금
celebrate	보험
diplomatic	이익
applaud	축하하다
criticize	환율(교환 비율)
opposite	기념일
respect	예측하다. 예언하다
despise	박수치다, 찬사를 보내다
financial	분석가
analyst	비판하다
predict	재정적인
exchange rate	반대(의)
benefit	경멸하다
insurance	존경(하다)
pension	외교적인

▶ ___ 채우기

사라져갔다 ➡ faded _____

찬사받았다 ➡ has _____ applauded

당분간 ➡ for the time _____

* 지금껏 발견되었던 가장 큰 **nest**는 무게가 1톤입니다. 대머리 독수리는 실제로 대머리가 아닙니다.

  ➜ .... 친 단어의 뜻은?
  ① 동굴　　　　　② 둥지

  The heaviest **nest** ever found is one ton! Bald eagles aren't actually bald.

* 상어의 입질은 순식간에 그녀의 수영복을 찢었고 상어의 이빨이 그녀의 피부를 **penetrated**.

  ➜ .... 친 단어의 뜻은?
  ① 마사지했다.　　　　② 관통했다.

  The shark's bite instantly ripped her wet suit and the shark teeth **penetrated** her skin.

---

bald 대머리인　　rip 찢다　　bite 물어뜯기, 물다

* 예수는 **carpenter**였다.

➡ .... 친 단어의 뜻은?
① 목사   ② 목수

Jesus was a **carpenter**.

* 무고한 사람들은 순찰하는 경찰관이 불심검문을 하면 **offended** 할 수도 있다.

➡ .... 친 단어의 뜻은?
① 친절한   ② 불쾌한

Innocent people might feel **offended** if they are questioned by a patrolling policeperson.

innocent 죄 없는, 순진한   patrol 순찰(하다)

* 죄수들의 팔다리는 잘려졌다. 그리고 그들의 시신은 **ditch**에 버려졌다.

➡ .... 친 단어의 뜻은?
① 병원   ② 도랑

The prisoners' arms and legs had been cut off and
their bodies thrown into the **ditch**.

흐름상 이 자리에 had been이 생략되었습니다.

* **Bald** 독수리는 곡물 밭을 망치는 설치류 동물들을 잡아먹어 인간에게 도움
을 줍니다.

➡ .... 친 단어의 뜻은?
① 귀여운   ② 대머리

Bald eagles help humans by catching rodents that destroy
grain fields.

cut off 잘라내다   rodent 설치류(쥐)   destroy 파괴하다

TEST 17 복습

▶ 단어 연결하기

nest	• •	순수한, 무고한
bald	• •	목수
shark	• •	불쾌한
instantly	• •	순찰(하다)
penetrate	• •	관통하다
carpenter	• •	죄수
innocent	• •	도랑
offended	• •	둥지
patrol	• •	파괴하다
prisoner	• •	설치류 동물
ditch	• •	대머리
rodent	• •	상어
destroy	• •	순식간에, 즉시

▶ ___ 채우기

지금껏 발견된 ➡ ever _____

순찰하는 경찰관 ➡ a _____ policeperson

잘려졌다 ➡ had been _____ off

* 세종대왕은 한문이 **literacy**를 저하시킴을 깨달았다.

➡ .... 친 단어의 뜻은?
  ① 식욕　　　　　② 읽고 쓰는 능력

King Sejong recognized that Chinese characters discouraged
literacy.

* 지적장애인들은 그들이 **sympathy**가 아니라 공동체의식을 원한다고 말한다.

➡ .... 친 단어의 뜻은?
  ① 무시　　　　　② 동정심

<the+형용사>는 <~한 사람들>로 해석될 때가 많다.

The mentally disabled say they want a sense of community, not
sympathy.

recognize 깨닫다, 인식하다　　courage 용기　　encourage (용기를)북돋우다
discourage (용기를)잃게하다

* 그는 일본과는 반대로 독일을 대표해서 전쟁 희생자들에게 **forgiveness**를
빌었다.

➡ .... 친 단어의 뜻은?
① 인내   ② 용서

He asked for **forgiveness** from the war victims on behalf of
Germany in the opposite of Japan.

* 그녀는 **good deeds**에 대해 칭찬을 받아 마땅하다.

➡ .... 친 단어의 뜻은?
① 악행   ② 선행

She deserves praising for **good deeds**.

on behalf of ~를 대표해서, ~를 대신해서   deserve ~할 가치가 있다

* 국산은 말할 것도 없이 **중국산보다 더 싼 프랑스산 빨래바구니를 한국 retailers**가 팔고 있다.

➡ .... 친 단어의 뜻은?
　① 소매치기　　　② 소매상인

Korean **retailers** sell French—made laundry baskets that are cheaper than Chinese products not to mention Korean ones.

* 고등학교 동창회에 모인 사람들은 옛 시절에 대한 **nostalgia**에 젖었다.

➡ .... 친 단어의 뜻은?
　① 봄비　　　　　② 향수

People at the high school reunion were filled with **nostalgia** about old times.

laundry 빨래, 세탁　　　reunion 동창회, 재회

TEST 18 복습

▶ 단어 연결하기

recognize •	• 깨닫다, 인정하다
discourage •	• 읽고 쓰는 능력
literacy •	• 행위
sympathy •	• 향수
forgiveness •	• 낙담시키다, 저하시키다
victim •	• 동정
deserve •	• 칭찬하다
praise •	• 동창회, 재결합
deed •	• 용서
retailer •	• 희생자
laundry •	• ~할 가치가 있다
reunion •	• 소매상인
nostalgia •	• 빨래

▶ ___ 채우기

지적장애인들 ➡ the mentally _____

독일을 대표해서 ➡ on _____ of Germany

국산은 말할 것도 없이 ➡ not to _____ Korean ones

STEP 19

* 심리학자와 정신과 의사 모두 환자를 상담하지만 약처방은 **psychiatrist**만 할 수 있다.

➡ _____ 친 단어의 뜻은?
　① 심리학자　　　② 정신과 의사

> Both psychologists and psychiatrists counsel patients but only **psychiatrists** can prescribe medication.

* 사이버위기 경보단계는 정상 · 관심 · 주의 · **Alert** · 심각으로 분류된다.

➡ _____ 친 단어의 뜻은?
　① 산만　　　② 경계

> Cyber Alert Crisis levels are classified as Normal － Attention － Caution － **Alert** － Serious.

prescribe 처방하다　　medication 약물　　classify 분류하다

* 그는 애완동물들이 배고픔이 아니라 지루함, **anxiety**, 우울감 같은 스트레스에 대한 반응으로 많이 먹는다는 것을 발견했다.

➡ .... 친 단어의 뜻은?
① 돌봄　　　　　② 걱정

> He discovered that pets eat too much, not due to hunger, but in response to stress, like boredom, **anxiety** and depression.

* 제가 당신에게 **infection**을 막기 위해서 항생제는 처방해 드리지요.

➡ .... 친 단어의 뜻은?
① 지출　　　　　② 감염

> I'll prescribe some antibiotics for you to prevent **infection**.

boredom 지루함　　　antibiotic 항생제　　　prevent 예방하다

* 직독직해 10대들에게 성생활이 잘못된 것이라고 가르치는 것은 / 그들은 믿게 강요한다. / 그들의 자연스러운 성적 **impulses**가 나쁘다고 / 그리고 그것은 큰 혼란과 자기회의를 초래할 수 있다.

➜ .... 친 단어의 뜻은?
  ① 향상   ② 충동

Teaching teens that sex is wrong / forces them to believe / that their natural sexual **impulses** are wrong, / which can cause great confusion and self–doubt.

* 비교하면 은메달은 93퍼센트의 **silver**와 7퍼센트의 구리로 구성되어 있다.

➜ .... 친 단어의 뜻은?
  ① 금   ② 은

In comparison the silver medal is made up of 93 percent silver and 7 percent copper.

---

confusion 혼란   be made up of ~로 구성되다   copper 구리

TEST 19 복습

▶ 단어 연결하기

psychologist	• •	구리
psychiatrist	• •	혼란
prescribe	• •	충동
crisis	• •	감염
alert	• •	항생제
boredom	• •	걱정
anxiety	• •	지루함
antibiotics	• •	경계(하는)
infection	• •	위기
impulse	• •	처방하다
confusion	• •	정신과 의사
copper	• •	심리학자
be made up of	• •	~로 구성되다

▶ ___ 채우기

분류되다 ➡ are _____

스트레스에 대한 반응으로 ➡ in _____ to stress

비교하면 ➡ ____ comparison

* 아기들은 손과 무릎으로 <u>crawl</u>.

➡ .... 친 단어의 뜻은?
① 청소한다.   ② 기어다닌다.

Babies **crawl** on their hands and knees.

* 수술 후에 무릎을 다시 강하게 하기 위해 <u>rehabilitate</u> 해야 할 것이다.

➡ .... 친 단어의 뜻은?
① 생활하다.   ② 재활하다.

After surgery he would have to **rehabilitate** <u>the knee</u> to make it strong again.

surgery 수술   knee 무릎

* 아산의료센터의 의사들은 그의 아버지가 liver암 때문에 곧 이식 수술을 할 필요가 있다고 결정했다.

→ .... 친 단어의 뜻은?
① 유방 　　　　② 간

> Doctors from Asan Medical Center determined that his father needed to have transplant surgery soon because of his **liver** cancer.

* 그의 심장, 간, lungs 그리고 두 신장이 같은 날 다섯 명의 다른 환자들에게 이식되었다.

→ .... 친 단어의 뜻은?
① 뇌 　　　　② 폐

> His heart, liver, **lungs** and two kidneys were transplanted to five different patients on the same day.

determine 결정하다 　　　transplant 이식(하다)

93

* 같은 해, 그 도시는 자전거 대여 프로그램을 도입하여 시의 **transportation** 문화를 바꿨다.

→ .... 친 단어의 뜻은?
　① 고통　　　　　② 교통(운송)

> The same year the city launched a bike—rental program, changing its **transportation** culture.

* 8월 22일 다목적 **satellite** 아리랑 5호가 성공적으로 발사되었다.

→ .... 친 단어의 뜻은?
　① 댐　　　　　② 위성

> On August 22, the multipurpose **satellite** Arirang 5 was launched successfully.

launch 착수하다, 발사하다　　　multipurpose 다목적의

TEST 20 복습

▶ **단어 연결하기**

crawl	• •	기어다니다
knee	• •	위성
surgery	• •	간
rehabilitate	• •	재활하다
determine	• •	무릎
transplant	• •	착수하다
liver	• •	폐
lung	• •	이식(하다)
kidney	• •	결정하다
launch	• •	운송, 교통
transportation	• •	수술
multipurpose	• •	신장
satellite	• •	다목적의

▶ **___ 채우기**

(그것을) 강하게 하기 위해 ➡ to make it _____

이식되었다 ➡ were _____

발사되었다 ➡ was _____

STEP 16

+ The ship faded away below the horizon.
+ Korea and Australia are currently celebrating their 50th anniversary of diplomatic relations.
+ His action has been applauded by a few but criticized by many others.
+ The opposite words of respect are to despise and hate.
+ Financial analysts across the world predict the current won-dollar exchange rate to continue for the time being.
+ The company offers benefits such as health insurance, pensions and employee discounts.

STEP 17

+ The heaviest nest ever found is one ton! Bald eagles aren't actually bald.
+ The shark's bite instantly ripped her wet suit and the shark teeth penetrated her skin.
+ Jesus was a carpenter.
+ Innocent people might feel offended if they are questioned by a patrolling policeperson.
+ The prisoners' arms and legs had been cut off and their bodies thrown into the ditch.
+ Bald eagles help humans by catching rodents that destroy grain fields.

STEP 18

+ King Sejong recognized that Chinese characters discouraged literacy.
+ The mentally disabled say they want a sense of community, not sympathy.
+ He asked for forgiveness from the war victims on behalf of Germany in the opposite of Japan.

- + She deserves praising for good deeds.
- + Korean retailers sell French-made laundry baskets that are cheaper than Chinese products not to mention Korean ones.
- + People at the high school reunion were filled with nostalgia about old times.

STEP 19

- + Both psychologists and psychiatrists counsel patients but only psychiatrists can prescribe medication.
- + Cyber Alert Crisis levels are classified as Normal–Attention–Caution–Alert–Serious.
- + He discovered that pets eat too much, not due to hunger, but in response to stress, like boredom, anxiety and depression.
- + I'll prescribe some antibiotics for you to prevent infection.
- + Teaching teens that sex is wrong forces them to believe that their natural sexual impulses are wrong, which can cause great confusion and self-doubt.
- + In comparison the silver medal is made up of 93 percent silver and 7 percent copper.

STEP 20

- + Babies crawl on their hands and knees.
- + After surgery he would have to rehabilitate the knee to make it strong again.
- + Doctors from Asan Medical Center determined that his father needed to have transplant surgery soon because of his liver cancer.
- + His heart, liver, lungs and two kidneys were transplanted to five different patients on the same day.
- + The same year the city launched a bike-rental program, changing its transportation culture.
- + On August 22, the multipurpose satellite Arirang 5 was launched successfully.

STEP 21

* 사람들은 그 물귀신의 주된 목적이 사람들을 위험한 물속으로 유혹해서 그들을 **drown** 하는 것이라고 믿는다.

　➡　........................ 친 단어의 뜻은?
　　① 잠수하다.　　　② 익사시키다.

> People believe that the water ghost's main purpose is to lure people into dangerous water and then **drown** them.

* 그는 일제 **colonial** 기간 동안 한국 문화를 보존하는 데 헌신했습니다.

　➡　........................ 친 단어의 뜻은?
　　① 단속　　　　② 식민지(의)

> be dedicated to ~ing: ~에 헌신하다
> to 다음에 동사원형이 아니라 동명사(~ing)가 오는 것에 주의하세요.

> He was dedicated to preserving Korean culture during the Japanese **colonial** era.

---

lure 유혹하다　　preserve 보존하다　　era 기간, 시대

98

* 우리는 모든 사람들에게 교육 재원이 **evenly** 배분되지 않는 세계에서 산다.

➡ .... 친 단어의 뜻은?
  ① 부족하게   ② 균등하게

We live in a world where educational and financial resources are not **evenly** distributed among all people.

* **Marine** 동물들이 상승하는 바다의 온도 때문에 위험에 처해 있다.

➡ .... 친 단어의 뜻은?
  ① 애완(의)   ② 바다(의)

Marine animals are at risk because of the rising temperatures of the sea.

distribute 배분하다   temperature 온도

* 최악의 **drought** 때문에 북한 사람들은 영양실조와 굶주림의 위기에 처해 있습니다.

➡ .... 친 단어의 뜻은?
   ① 지진   ② 가뭄

Due to the worst **drought**, North Koreans are at risk of malnutrition and starvation.

* **Mars**와 금성도 이전에는 바닷물이 있었을지도 모른다.

➡ .... 친 단어의 뜻은?
   ① (경기도)화성   ② 화성

Mars and Venus may have had water oceans in the past.

malnutrition 영양실조   starvation 굶주림
may have p.p ～였을지도 모른다(과거의 추측)

100

TEST 21 복습

▶ 단어 연결하기

ghost	기간, 시대
purpose	분배하다, 배포하다
lure	목적
drown	화성
preserve	유혹하다
colonial	균등하게
era	영양실조
distribute	가뭄
evenly	식민지의
marine	익사하다
drought	바다의
malnutrition	보존하다
Mars	유령

▶ ___ 채우기

보존하는 데 헌신했다 ➡ was _____ to preserving

위험에 처해있다 ➡ are ___ risk

바닷물이 있었을지도 모른다 ➡ may have _____ water oceans

101

* 나는 담배를 끊었는데 지금 담배가 피우고 싶어 못 견디겠어요. 그 **temptation**을 극복하는게 어려워요.

→ .... 친 단어의 뜻은?

① 냄새   ② 유혹

> I quit smoking. But I'm dying for a cigarette right now. I'm having a hard time getting over the **temptation**.

* 한국인들은 **conservative**와 중도, 진보 사이에 어떤 차이가 있는지 알지 못할지도 모른다.

→ .... 친 단어의 뜻은?

① 수리   ② 보수(의)

> Koreans might not know what the difference is between a **conservative**, moderate and liberal.

---

get over 극복하다, 회복하다   moderate 온건한, 온건주의자
liberal 진보적인, 진보주의자

* 한때 찬란했던 아즈텍과 마야 문명은 자신들의 유적을 전달할 수단인 글자
  가 없었기 때문에 거의 흔적없이 **perished**.

→ .... 친 단어의 뜻은?
  ① 소생했다.　　　　② 소멸했다.

> Once-glorious Aztecan and Mayan civilizations **perished**
> without much trace because they did not have letters to pass
> down their heritage with.

* 이것은 개가 **sheep**, 소, 염소 또는 말보다 훨씬 이전에 길들여진 최초의 동
  물임을 증명한다.

→ .... 친 단어의 뜻은?
  ① 용　　　　　　　② 양

> This proves that dogs were the first animals to be domesticated,
> long before **sheep**, cows, goats or horses.

---

civilization 문명　　　pass down 전달하다, 물려주다　　　heritage 유적, 유물
domesticate 길들이다

＊ 대개 병원 의사나 간호사들은 소변 채취 시 환자와 **accompany** 하지 않는다.

➡ .... 친 단어의 뜻은?
　① 연행하다　　　② 동행하다

Normally doctors or nurses in hospitals do not **accompany** patients in collecting urine samples.

＊ 용의자를 체포하기 위해 **warrant**가 발부되었다.

➡ .... 친 단어의 뜻은?
　① 초대장　　　② 영장

A **warrant** was issued for the suspect's arrest.

urine 소변, 오줌　　　suspect 용의자, 의심하다

TEST 22 복습

▶ 단어 연결하기

get over	극복하다
temptation	양
conservative	중도, 온건한
moderate	유혹
liberal	체포(하다)
glorious	영장
perish	보수(의), 보수주의자
heritage	유산
prove	진보의, 진보주의자
domesticate	찬란한
sheep	오줌
accompany	동행하다
urine	증명하다
warrant	길들이다
arrest	소멸하다

▶ ___ 채우기

담배가 피우고 싶어 못 견디겠다 ➡ am _____ for a cigarette

거의 흔적 없이 ➡ _____ much trace

길들여진 ➡ to be _____

발부되었다 was _____

* 차이점은 제쳐두고 **compromise**에 도달하도록 노력하자.

➡ .... 친 단어의 뜻은?
① 정상   ② 타협

> Let's lay aside our differences and try to reach a **compromise**.

* 한국은 약 2,500명의 군인들을 이라크를 포함한 8곳의 군사 분쟁지역에 **dispatched**.

➡ .... 친 단어의 뜻은?
① 여행했다.   ② 파병했다.

> Korea **dispatched** about 2,500 soldiers to 8 military conflicts, including Iraq.

lay aside 제쳐두다, 일시중단하다   conflict 분쟁, 갈등

＊ 사람들과 마찬가지로 개 역시 나이를 먹음에 따라 **physical** 또는 정신적으로 병에 걸려 괴로워한다.

➜ .... 친 단어의 뜻은?
　① 구체적　　　　② 육체적

> In the same way as people, dogs suffer from both **physical** or mental illness as they age.

> 여기서 age는 문장 구조상 명사가 아니고 동사입니다.

＊ 계속되는 식량 부족에도 불구하고, 북한은 **luxury goods**의 수입을 늘렸습니다.

➜ .... 친 단어의 뜻은?
　① 곡물　　　　② 사치품

> Despite its continuous food shortages, North Korea has increased imports of **luxury goods**.

age 나이, 나이를 먹다　　　shortage 부족　　　import 수입(하다)

* 1947년 여름, 뉴멕시코 주 로즈웰의 주민들이 하늘에서 떨어지는 이상한 물체를 **witnessed**.

　➡　.......................... 친 단어의 뜻은?
　　① 구입했다.　　　② 목격했다.

> In the summer of 1947, residents of Roswell, New Mexico, **witnessed** a strange object falling from the sky.

* 그녀와 결혼하려고 했는데 그녀의 가족이 **objected**.

　➡　.......................... 친 단어의 뜻은?
　　① 울었다.　　　② 반대했다.

> I was planning to marry her, but her family **objected**.

　　marry는 '~와 결혼하다'입니다.
　　그래서 marry with는 어색한 표현입니다.

resident 주민　　　object 물체, 반대하다

108

TEST 23 복습

▶ **단어 연결하기**

lay aside •		• 물체, 반대하다
compromise •		• 목격하다, 목격자
dispatch •		• 파병하다
conflict •		• 부족
military •		• 제쳐두다
suffer from •		• 주민
physical •		• 육체적인
shortage •		• ~로 고통받다
luxury •		• 군대의
resident •		• 타협하다
witness •		• 분쟁
object •		• 사치의

▶ **___ 채우기**

사람들과 마찬가지로 → in the _____ way ___ people

계속되는 식량 부족에도 불구하고 → _____ its continuous food shortages

하늘에서 떨어지는 → _____ from the sky

* 곡식과 과일이 논밭과 **orchards**에서 익어가고 있다.

➜ .... 친 단어의 뜻은?
 ① 냉장고 　　　② 과수원

Grains and fruits are ripening in the fields and **orchards**.

* 아직도 우리 사회에는 동성애자들에 대한 강한 **bias**가 남아 있다.

➜ .... 친 단어의 뜻은?
 ① 애정 　　　② 편견

There remains an intense **bias** against homosexuals in our society.

ripen 익다　　　intense 강한, 집중적인

* <u>autopsy</u>는 그의 죽음을 약물 과용 때문인 것으로 결론내렸다.

➡ .... 친 단어의 뜻은?
　① 마취　　　　② 부검

The **autopsy** concluded that his death resulted from an overdose of drugs.

* 남에게 뒤지지 않으려고 애쓰다 <u>debt</u>까지 졌다.

➡ .... 친 단어의 뜻은?
　① 빗　　　　② 빚

He got into **debt** trying to keep up with the joneses.

conclude 결론내리다　　result from ~때문이다　　dose 복용
overdose 과다복용　　keep up with ~를 따라잡다

* 그녀는 벽에 붙여놓은 **comb**을 떼어내 머리를 빗습니다.

➜ .... 친 단어의 뜻은?
 ① 효자손 ② 빗

She takes a **comb** which is attached to the wall and combs her hair.

여기서 combs는 흐름상 동사입니다.

* 경찰은 군중을 해산시키고 시위를 더 이상 하지 못하게 하려고 **brutal** 최루 가스와 물대포를 사용했다.

➜ .... 친 단어의 뜻은?
 ① 부드러운 ② 잔인한

Police have been using **brutal** tear gas and water canons to break up the crowds and deter further protesting.

---

comb 빗, 빗질하다 break up 해산하다, 헤어지다 deter 단념시키다

TEST 24 복습

▶ 단어 연결하기

grain •	• 부검
ripen •	• 편견
orchard •	• 부착하다, 붙이다
intense •	• 곡식
bias •	• 익다
autopsy •	• 시위하다, 항의하다
overdose •	• 과수원
debt •	• 단념시키다
comb •	• 잔인한
attach •	• 강력한
brutal •	• 과다복용
deter •	• 빚
protest •	• 빗

▶ ___ 채우기

~ 때문이었다 ➡ resulted _____

남에게 뒤지지 않으려고 ➡ to keep up with the _____

벽에 붙여놓은 ➡ which is _____ to the wall

* 칼슘은 뼈와 치아를 만들고 근육의 이완과 **contraction**에 중요한 역할을 한다.

➡ .... 친 단어의 뜻은?
① 팽창   ② 수축

Calcium play a critical role in bone and tooth formation and muscle relaxation and **contraction**.

* 우리 몸은 땀을 흘려서 **evaporation**을 통해 열을 방출시킬 수 있다.

➡ .... 친 단어의 뜻은?
① 흡수   ② 증발

Our bodies can sweat, thereby losing heat by **evaporation**.

critical 중요한, 결정적인   relaxation 이완, 휴식   sweat 땀, 땀을 흘리다

* 그렇다면 온도는 같은데 왜 **rural** 지역보다 도시 지역이 더 더울까?

➡ .... 친 단어의 뜻은?
① 열대우림   ② 시골(의)

If so, why is it that the urban areas are hotter than **rural** ones when the temperatures are the same?

* 외과의사들은 신경, 동맥, 정맥을 다시 붙일 때 정확도를 얻기 해 **microscope** 을 사용해야 한다.

➡ .... 친 단어의 뜻은?
① 돋보기   ② 현미경

Surgeons have to use a **microscope** to attain accuracy when reattaching nerves, arteries and veins.

urban 도시의   attain 얻다, 달성하다   artery 동맥

* 등산로가 너무 좁아서 등산객들이 **ascend**하거나 내려가기 위해 기다려야
 한다.

 ➡ .... 친 단어의 뜻은?
  ① 날다   ② 오르다

 Because the trail is so narrow, climbers have to wait for them
 to **ascend** or descend.

* 우리는 빈번히 현대 도시에서 사람들의 높은 주거 **density**를 당연한 것으
 로 여긴다.

 ➡ .... 친 단어의 뜻은?
  ① 밀당   ② 밀도

 Frequently, we take for granted the extreme **density** of human
 habitation in modern cities.

trail 오솔길, 등산로   habitation 주거, 서식지

TEST 25 복습

▶ 단어 연결하기

critical •	• 시골의
formation •	• 도시의
contraction •	• 중요한, 결정적인, 비판적인
sweat •	• 주거지
evaporation •	• 현미경
urban •	• 증발
rural •	• 밀도
surgeon •	• 형성
microscope •	• 수축
artery •	• 땀(을 흘리다)
trail •	• 외과의사
ascend •	• 오르다
density •	• 등산로, 오솔길
habitation •	• 동맥

▶ ___ 채우기

그렇다면 → if ___

다시 붙일 때 → when _____

당연한 것으로 여긴다 → take for _____

STEP 21

+ People believe that the water ghost's main purpose is to lure people into dangerous water and then drown them.

+ He was dedicated to preserving Korean culture during the Japanese colonial era.

+ We live in a world where educational and financial resources are not evenly distributed among all people.

+ Marine animals are at risk because of the rising temperatures of the sea.

+ Due to the worst drought, North Koreans are at risk of malnutrition and starvation.

+ Mars and Venus may have had water oceans in the past.

STEP 22

+ I quit smoking. But I'm dying for a cigarette right now. I'm having a hard time getting over the temptation.

+ Koreans might not know what the difference is between a conservative, moderate and liberal.

+ Once-glorious Aztecan and Mayan civilizations perished without much trace because they did not have letters to pass down their heritage with.

+ This proves that dogs were the first animals to be domesticated, long before sheep, cows, goats or horses.

+ Normally doctors or nurses in hospitals do not accompany patients in collecting urine samples.

+ A warrant was issued for the suspect's arrest.

STEP 23

+ Let's lay aside our differences and try to reach a compromise.

+ Korea dispatched about 2,500 soldiers to 8 military conflicts, including Iraq.

+ In the same way as people, dogs suffer from both physical or mental illness as they age.

+ Despite its continuous food shortages, North Korea has increased imports of luxury goods.
+ In the summer of 1947, residents of Roswell, New Mexico, witnessed a strange object falling from the sky.
+ I was planning to marry her, but her family objected.

STEP 24

+ Grains and fruits are ripening in the fields and orchards.
+ There remains an intense bias against homosexuals in our society.
+ The autopsy concluded that his death resulted from an overdose of drugs.
+ He got into debt trying to keep up with the joneses.
+ She takes a comb which is attached to the wall and combs her hair.
+ Police have been using brutal tear gas and water canons to break up the crowds and deter further protesting.

STEP 25

+ Calcium play a critical role in bone and tooth formation and muscle relaxation and contraction.
+ Our bodies can sweat, thereby losing heat by evaporation.
+ If so, why is it that the urban areas are hotter than rural ones when the temperatures are the same?
+ Surgeons have to use a microscope to attain accuracy when reattaching nerves, arteries and veins.
+ Because the trail is so narrow, climbers have to wait for them to ascend or descend.
+ Frequently, we take for granted the extreme density of human habitation in modern cities.

* 우리는 **objective** 입장에서 전달된 정확한 정보를 얻기 위해 신문을 읽는다.

➡ .... 친 단어의 뜻은?
　① 주관적인　　　　② 객관적인

> in order to ~ = so as to ~ : <~하기 위해서> 입니다.

We read newspapers in order to obtain accurate information delivered in an **objective** stance.

* 이 단체의 **objectives**는 민주주의와 개인의 자유를 증진시키고 질병과 가난에 싸우는 것이다.

➡ .... 친 단어의 뜻은?
　① 적　　　　　　② 목적

The **objectives** of this organization are to promote democracy, individual liberty and to fight against disease and poverty.

accurate 정확한　　stance 입장, 자세　　objective 객관적인, 목적
in order to(=so as to) ~하기 위하여　　promote 증진시키다, 홍보하다　　poverty 가난

＊ **Maturity**는 너가 몇 살 인지와 아무런 관련이 없다.

➡ .... 친 단어의 뜻은?
① 외모　　　　　② 성숙함

Maturity has nothing to do with how old you are.

＊ 식사에서 탄수화물과 당을 피하고 **fiber**가 풍부한 음식을 추가해라.

➡ .... 친 단어의 뜻은?
① 석유　　　　　② 섬유(질)

Avoid carbohydrates and sugars in the diet and add more **fiber** rich foods.

carbohydrate 탄수화물

* 지구의 상층 **atmosphere**에 있는 오존층은 위험한 자외선으로부터 우리를 보호해줍니다.

➡ .... 친 단어의 뜻은?
① 대기(기다림)　　　　② 대기

The ozone layer in the Earth's upper **atmosphere** protects us from dangerous ultraviolet light.

* 오랫동안 늑대들이 **fierce** 동물이라고 믿어왔지만 현실에서 그들은 인간을 거의 공격하지 않는다.

➡ .... 친 단어의 뜻은?
① 온순한　　　　② 사나운

Although wolves have long been believed to be **fierce** animals, they barely attack humans in reality.

layer 층, 지층　　　barely 거의 ~하지 않다

TEST 26 복습

▶ 단어 연결하기

obtain	• •	얻다
accurate	• •	정확한
objective	• •	객관적인, 목적
organization	• •	기관, 단체
poverty	• •	가난
maturity	• •	성숙함
carbohydrate	• •	탄수화물
fiber	• •	섬유(질)
atmosphere	• •	대기, 분위기
protect	• •	보호하다
ultraviolet	• •	자외선(의)
fierce	• •	사나운
barely	• •	거의 ~하지 않다

▶ ___ 채우기

얻기 위해 → in _____ to obtain

~와 아무 관련이 없다 → has _____ to do _____

거의 공격하지 않는다 → _____ attack

* 어떤 책에 보니까 인간은 자기가 가진 것에 **content** 때가 가장 행복하다고 하더라.

➡ .... 친 단어의 뜻은?
① 교만한   ② 만족한

I read from a book that people are happy when they are **content** with what they have.

* 개인의 정보를 사람의 **consent** 없이 수집하는 것은 심각한 사생활 침해다.

➡ .... 친 단어의 뜻은?
① 인지   ② 동의

Collecting personal information without the **consent** of the person is a serious privacy violation.

serious 심각한   violation 침해, 위반

＊ 학생들은 **geography** 시간에 몇몇 다른 도시의 경도를 찾으라는 요구를 받았다.

➜ .... 친 단어의 뜻은?
① 철학　　　　　② 지리(학)

The students were asked to find the longitude of several different cities in their **geography** class.

＊ 크리스마스에 친절과 온정이 세계 곳곳에서 **overflow**.

➜ .... 친 단어의 뜻은?
① 증발하다.　　　　② 넘쳐흐르다.

On Christmas, kindness and compassion **overflow** in every corner of the world.

longitude 경도　　　compassion 온정, 동정

125

* 최근 대한민국의 청년 **unemployment** 30만 명이 넘어섰으며 젊은 사람들은 절박한 심정으로 일자리를 구하고 있다.

➜ .... 친 단어의 뜻은?

① 창업(이)   ② 실업(이)

Recently youth **unemployment** rose above 300,000 in Korea and young people are desperately struggling to find jobs.

* **Definition**에 의하면 과학은 새롭고 실용적인 해결책을 만들기 위한 체계적인 방법에서의 지식의 축적이다.

➜ .... 친 단어의 뜻은?

① 종교   ② 정의

By **definition** science is the accumulation of knowledge in a systematic method to create new and practical solutions.

desperately 절박하게, 필사적으로   struggle 애쓰다, 투쟁하다
accumulation 축적, 누적   practical 실용적인, 실제적인

TEST 27 복습

▶ 단어 연결하기

content ·	· 온정, 동정
consent ·	· 경도
serious ·	· 축적
violation ·	· 만족한
longitude ·	· 동의(하다)
geography ·	· 방법
compassion ·	· 지리(학)
overflow ·	· 침해, 위반
unemployment ·	· 심각한, 진지한
desperately ·	· 정의
struggle ·	· 넘쳐흐르다
definition ·	· 실업
accumulation ·	· 절박하게
method ·	· 애쓰다, 투쟁하다

▶ ＿＿ 채우기

자기가(그들이) 가진 것 → ＿＿＿＿＿＿ they have

요구를 받았다 → were ＿＿＿＿＿＿

* 그의 조상 중 하나는 대서양을 지배했던 **notorious** 해적이었다.

→ .... 친 단어의 뜻은?
  ① 자상한   ② 악명 높은

One of his forefathers was a **notorious** pirate who predominated over the Atlantic Ocean.

* **Bribes**을 받거나 학생의 성적을 고치는 교사들도 같은 처벌에 직면할 것이다.

→ .... 친 단어의 뜻은?
  ① 기부   ② 뇌물

Teachers who take **bribes** and change student's grades will also face the same punishment.

* 정규직들이 **privileges**를 강화하는 것도 청년들의 취업 기회를 빼앗는다.

→ .... 친 단어의 뜻은?
① 양보　　　　② 특권

Reinforcing the **privileges** of permanent staff is also depriving youth of job opportunities.

deprive A of B: A에게서 B를 빼앗다.

* 나는 Tom처럼 **considerate** 사람을 승진시키지 않고 저런 비열한 사람같은 Harold를 승진시키다니 믿을 수 없어요.

→ .... 친 단어의 뜻은?
① 배가 나온　　　② 배려심 있는

I can't believe they didn't promote a **considerate** guy like Tom and instead promoted that creep Harold.

reinforce 강화하다　　　permanent 영원한　　　promote 승진시키다, 촉진하다
creep (명)네발로 기기, 비열한 사람 / (동)기어가다

* 그녀는 **terminal** 암을 진단받았을 때 희망을 잃었지만 5살밖에 되지 않은 그녀의 어린 아들이 그녀에게 다시 희망을 품을 수 있도록 격려한다.

➡ .... 친 단어의 뜻은?
① 초기(의)   ② 말기(의)

> 글의 흐름상 그녀가 진단하는게 아니라 진단받기 때문에 수동태가 자연스럽습니다. 그리고 주어(she)와 be동사(was)가 생략되었습니다.

She lost hope when diagnosed with **terminal** cancer but her young son, who only has 5 years to live, inspires her to hope again.

* 교통 **congestion**과 자동차 공해는 도시인들의 피할 수 없는 일상의 일부가 되었다.

➡ .... 친 단어의 뜻은?
① 혁명   ② 혼잡

Traffic **congestion** and car pollution have become an unavoidable part of life for urbanites.

> avoid(피하다), avoidable(피할 수 있는), unavoidable(피할 수 없는)

diagnose 진단하다   inspire 격려하다, 영감을 주다   pollution 공해
urbanite 도시인

130

TEST 28 복습

▶ **단어 연결하기**

forefather	• •	조상
notorious	• •	해적
pirate	• •	처벌
bribe	• •	특권
punishment	• •	기회
reinforce	• •	사려깊은, 배려심 있는
privilege	• •	격려하다, 영감을 주다
deprive	• •	피할 수 없는
opportunity	• •	혼잡
promote	• •	말기의
considerate	• •	승진시키다
terminal	• •	빼앗다
inspire	• •	강화하다
congestion	• •	뇌물
unavoidable	• •	악명 높은

▶ **___ 채우기**

저런 비열한 사람같은 Harold ➡ _____ creep Harold

진단받았을 때 ➡ when _____

* 만약 강아지들이 충분히 훈련을 받는다면, 그들은 그들의 **paws**로 그것을 눌러 세탁기를 열고, 옷을 운반하고, 세탁기를 켜기 위해 짖을 수 있습니다.

→ .... 친 단어의 뜻은?
① 손 ② (동물의) 발

If dogs are fully trained, they can open the washing machine by pushing it with their **paws**, load the clothes and bark to turn it on.

> 대명사는 꼭 동사와 부사 사이에 위치합니다.
> 대명사(it)의 위치에 유의하세요.

* 추가로 **lizards**는 꼬리의 여러 곳에서 재생하는 세포 조직이 있다.

→ .... 친 단어의 뜻은?
① 도마 ② 도마뱀

Additionally, **lizards** have cell tissues that grow back in multiple locations of the tails.

> back이 동사와 연결되면 '다시'로 해석될 때가 많습니다.

---

load 운반하다, 짐 bark 짖다 multiple 다양한, 다수의 location 위치

* 인질은 그의 가족이 10만 달러 **ransom**을 지불하고 나서 인질범들로부터 풀려났다.

➡ .... 친 단어의 뜻은?
   ① 근사값   ② 몸값

The hostage was released by his captors after his family paid a $100,000 **ransom.**

* 정치는 국가를 위해 개인의 이기심과 **altruism** 사이에서 접점을 찾아내는 것이다.

➡ .... 친 단어의 뜻은?
   ① 이율배반   ② 이타심

Politics is finding points of contact between individual greed and **altruism** for the nation.

hostage 인질   captor 인질범, 포획자   politics 정치(학)
greed 이기심, 탐욕

* 이순신 장군은 두려움과 싸우면서 나라와 자신이 직면한 수많은 **adversities**
에 처한 나라와 백성을 구했다.

  ➡ .... 친 단어의 뜻은?
  ① 역설   ② 역경

  > Admiral Yi saved his country and its people in a number of
  > **adversities** facing the country and himself while fighting fears.

* 내 상사는 나의 공정한 의견은 무시하고 자기 아들의 **unjust** 그리고 어리석
은 충고를 따랐다.

  ➡ .... 친 단어의 뜻은?
  ① 타당한   ② 부당한

  > prejudice(편견), prejudiced(편견을 가진),
  > unprejudiced(편견이 없는, 공정한)

  > My boss ignored my unprejudiced opinion and followed his son'
  > s **unjust** and foolish advice.

  > just는 '공정한'이라는 뜻도 있어요.

  ---
  fear 두려움   ignore 무시하다

TEST 29 복습

▶ 단어 연결하기

paw •	• (동물의)발
bark •	• 인질범
additionally •	• 부당한
lizard •	• 짖다
location •	• 몸값
hostage •	• 무시하다
captor •	• 추가적으로
ransom •	• 인질
politics •	• 두려움
greed •	• 도마뱀
altruism •	• 역경
adversity •	• 위치
fear •	• 이타심
ignore •	• 이기심, 탐욕
unjust •	• 정치(학)

▶ ___ 채우기

재생하는 세포 조직 ➡ cell tissues that _____ back

수많은 역경 ➡ a _____ of adversities

* 온수로 샤워하는 것은 관절염, <u>muscle tears</u>와 관련된 관절통증을 완화해 준다.

  ➡ ·················· 친 단어의 뜻은?
    ① 근육 눈물 　　　　　　② 근육 파열

  Showering with hot water eases joint pain associated with arthritis, **muscle tears**.

* 이것은 광범위한 연대와 창조적이고 <u>persistent</u> 노력을 요구하는 어려운 과제이다.

  ➡ ·················· 친 단어의 뜻은?
    ① 지겨운 　　　　② 지속적인

  This is a difficult challenge that calls for wide collaboration and creative, **persistent** efforts.

---

ease 완화하다, 편해지다, 편함　　arthritis 관절염　　call for 요구하다
collaboration 연대, 협력

* 이를 위해 서울과 워싱턴은 동맹을 공고히 하고 **collaboration**을 증진시켜야 한다.

➡ .... 친 단어의 뜻은?
① 분열　　　　　② 협력

For this, Seoul and Washington must solidify their alliance and set up **collaboration**.

* 많은 노인들은 소리를 **to amplify** 보청기를 사용한다.

➡ .... 친 단어의 뜻은?
① 줄이기 위해　　　　　② 증폭하기 위해

Many elderly people use hearing aids **to amplify** sounds.

solid 고체, 단단한　　solidify 응고시키다, 단단하게 하다　　alliance 동맹

* 한국 농민들은 시장 개방은 결국 국내산 쌀에 대한 수요가 사라질 것이라고 **contend**.

➡ _____ 친 단어의 뜻은?
① 기대한다.　　　② 주장한다.

Korean farmers **contend** the opening of the market would eventually kill demand for domestic rice.

* 그러나 그는 최저임금 인상이 실제로 고용을 늘린다고 **asserts**.

➡ _____ 친 단어의 뜻은?
① 항의한다.　　　② 주장한다.

But he **asserts** that increases in minimum wage actually increase employment.

domestic 국내의　　　increase 증가, 인상, 증가하다　　　employment 고용

138

TEST 30 복습

▶ 단어 연결하기

ease •	• 동맹, 연합
arthritis •	• 완화하다, 편함
collaboration •	• 고용
persistent •	• 임금
solidify •	• 연대, 협력
alliance •	• 지원, 도움
aid •	• 관절염
amplify •	• 공고히 하다, 응고시키다
contend •	• 지속적인
demand •	• 수요, 요구(하다)
domestic •	• 증폭하다
assert •	• 주장하다
wage •	• 주장하다
employment •	• 국내의

▶ ___ 채우기

관절염과 관련된 ➡ _____ with arthritis

요구하는 어려운 과제 ➡ a difficult challenge that calls ____

STEP 26

+ We read newspapers in order to obtain accurate information delivered in an objective stance.

+ The objectives of this organization are to promote democracy, individual liberty and to fight against disease and poverty.

+ Maturity has nothing to do with how old you are.

+ Avoid carbohydrates and sugars in the diet and add more fiber rich foods.

+ The ozone layer in the Earth's upper atmosphere protects us from dangerous ultraviolet light.

+ Although wolves have long been believed to be fierce animals, they barely attack humans in reality.

STEP 27

+ I read from a book that people are happy when they are content with what they have.

+ Collecting personal information without the consent of the person is a serious privacy violation.

+ The students were asked to find the longitude of several different cities in their geography class.

+ On Christmas, kindness and compassion overflow in every corner of the world.

+ Recently youth unemployment rose above 300,000 in Korea and young people are desperately struggling to find jobs.

+ By definition science is the accumulation of knowledge in a systematic method to create new and practical solutions.

STEP 28

+ One of his forefathers was a notorious pirate who predominated over the Atlantic Ocean.

+ Teachers who take bribes and change student's grades will also face the same punishment.

+ Reinforcing the privileges of permanent staff is also depriving youth of job opportunities.

+ I can't believe they didn't promote a considerate guy like Tom and instead promoted that creep Harold.

+ She lost hope when diagnosed with terminal cancer but her young son, who only has 5 years to live, inspires her to hope again.

+ Traffic congestion and car pollution have become an unavoidable part of life for urbanites.

STEP 28

+ If dogs are fully trained, they can open the washing machine by pushing it with their paws, load the clothes and bark to turn it on.

+ Additionally, lizards have cell tissues that grow back in multiple locations of the tails.

+ The hostage was released by his captors after his family paid a $100,000 ransom.

+ Politics is finding points of contact between individual greed and altruism for the nation.

+ Admiral Yi saved his country and its people in a number of adversities facing the country and himself while fighting fears.

+ My boss ignored my unprejudiced opinion and followed his son's unjust and foolish advice.

STEP 30

+ Showering with hot water eases joint pain associated with arthritis, muscle tears.

+ This is a difficult challenge that calls for wide collaboration and creative, persistent efforts.

+ For this, Seoul and Washington must solidify their alliance and set up collaboration.

+ Many elderly people use hearing aids to amplify sounds.

+ Korean farmers contend the opening of the market would eventually kill demand for domestic rice.

+ But he asserts that increases in minimum wage actually increase employment.

* 외교관들은 영어에 **proficient** 해야 하는데 이것이 전세계적으로 사용되는 글로벌 언어이기 때문이다.

→ .... 친 단어의 뜻은?
① 미숙한　　　　② 능숙한

Diplomats should be **proficient** in English, as it is the global language used around the world.

* 폐렴은 폐의 **inflammation** 또는 감염이다.

→ .... 친 단어의 뜻은?
① 염색　　　　② 염증

Pneumonia is an infection or **inflammation** of the lungs.

diplomat **외교관**　　　pneumonia **폐렴**

* 직독직해 작년에 / 14만 건의 교통사고는 발생했다. / negligence 때문에 / 전방주시의 / 그리고 전체 교통사고의 63%를 차지했다.

➡ _____ 친 단어의 뜻은?
① 분만   ② 태만

Last year, / 140,000 traffic accidents occurred / due to **negligence** / in keeping eyes forward, / accounting for 63 percent of all traffic accidents.

<, ~ing> 형태는 분사구문으로 대체로 "그리고 ~하다"로 해석됩니다.

* 역사를 공부하지 않은 사람들은 잘못된 역사적 **analogies**를 하는 경향이 있다.

➡ _____ 친 단어의 뜻은?
① 회상   ② 비유, 유추

People who don't study history are prone to bad historical **analogies**.

accident 사건, 사고   account for (숫자를)차지하다, (원인을) 설명하다
prone ~하는 경향이 있는, ~하기 쉬운

143

* 뱀이 물면 문자 그대로 뱀이 천천히 삼킬 수 있도록 잡힌 동물(동물희생자)를 **paralyze.**

➜ .... 친 단어의 뜻은?
  ① 안아준다   ② 마비시킨다

Snake bites literally **paralyze** the animal victim to allow the snake to swallow it slowly.

* 직독직해 세 명의 남자와 여섯 살짜리 소녀는 지금 안전하다. / 구조되고 나서 / 작은 배에서 / **adrift** 해왔던 / 멕시코 만에서 / 이틀 동안

➜ .... 친 단어의 뜻은?
  ① 여행하는   ② 표류하는

Three man and a six–year–old girl are safe now / after being rescued / from their tiny boat / which had been **adrift** / in the Gulf of Mexico / for two days.

---

literally 문자 그대로   victim 희생자   swallow 삼키다   rescue 구조하다

TEST 31 복습

▶ 단어 연결하기

diplomat	• •	외교관
proficient	• •	폐렴
pneumonia	• •	유추, 비유
inflammation	• •	마비시키다
lung	• •	표류하는
accident	• •	작은
negligence	• •	능숙한
analogy	• •	염증
literally	• •	삼키다
paralyze	• •	문자 그대로
swallow	• •	폐
tiny	• •	태만
adrift	• •	사건

▶ ___ 채우기

그리고 63%를 차지했다 ➡ , _____ for 63 percent

~하는 경향이 있다 ➡ are _____ to~

구조되고 나서 ➡ after being _____

* **Receipt** 원본을 주시면 가게에서 전액 환불을 해드립니다.

➡ .... 친 단어의 뜻은?
① 사진   ② 영수증

> The store can give you a full refund provided you show us the original **receipt**.

> provided 다음에 (주어, 동사-) 문장이 오면
> 조건 접속사 if와 같다.

* 새 충전기는 시장에 나와 있는 거의 모든 휴대전화와 **compatible** 있다.

➡ .... 친 단어의 뜻은?
① 사교성이 있는   ② 호환성이 있는

> The new charger is **compatible** with almost all types of cell phones in the market.

refund 환불(하다)   charger 충전지

* 수학, **astronomy**, 물리학에 소질이 있던 마크는 어렸을 때 컴퓨터 프로그래밍에 관심을 가졌다.

➡ .... 친 단어의 뜻은?
　① 국문학　　　　② 천문학

> Mark, who was excellent at math, **astronomy** and physics, was interested in computer programming as a child.

* 패스트푸드는 필수 영양소가 **deficient**하다.

➡ .... 친 단어의 뜻은?
　① 풍부한　　　　② 부족한

> Fast food is **deficient** in essential nutrients.

physics 물리학　　　essential 필수적인, 본질적인

* 　직독직해　 Thunder와 번개는 대략 비슷한 시간에 발생한다./비록 당신은
번개의 번쩍임을 보지만/ thunder 소리를 듣기 전에

➡ .... 친 단어의 뜻은?
　① 우박　　　　　　② 천둥

> Thunder and lightning occur at roughly the same time, /
> although you see the flash of lightning / before you hear the
> thunder.

* 피카소는 유산으로 수천 점의 예술 작품을 남긴 prolific 화가였다.

➡ .... 친 단어의 뜻은?
　① 극소수(의)　　　　　② 다작(의)

> Picasso was a prolific artist who left thousands of works of art
> as his legacy.

---

lightning 번개　　　　flash 번쩍임, 섬광, 번쩍이다　　　legacy 유산, 유물

TEST 32 복습

▶ 단어 연결하기

refund	•	•	유산
receipt	•	•	다작의
charger	•	•	번개
compatible	•	•	천둥
astronomy	•	•	영양소
physics	•	•	부족한
deficient	•	•	물리학
nutrient	•	•	천문학
thunder	•	•	호환할 수 있는
lightning	•	•	충전기
prolific	•	•	영수증
legacy	•	•	환불

▶ ___ 채우기

소질이 있던(뛰어났던) 마크 ➡ Mark, _____ was excellent

(그의) 유산으로 ➡ ___ his legacy

＊ 증대되는 **skepticism**에도 불구하고 한류로 알려진 현상은 최소한 패션과 화장품 산업에서 예상보다 더 길어질 수도 있다.

➡ .... 친 단어의 뜻은?
　① 산업화　　　② 회의론

> Despite growing **skepticism**, the phenomenon known as the Korean Wave might be longer than expected, at least in the fashion and cosmetics industries.

＊ 프랑스 회사들이 종업원들을 **to lay off** 또는 완전 해고한다는 것은 매우 어렵다.

➡ .... 친 단어의 뜻은?
　① 때리는 것　　② (일시) 해고하는 것

> It is very difficult for French corporations **to lay off** or fire employees.

---

phenomenon 현상　　　cosmetics 화장품　　　corporation (법인)회사
lay off (일시적으로) 해고하다

＊ 두 강 사이의 땅은 문명형성에 필수적인 **fertile** 땅이었다.

➡ .... 친 단어의 뜻은?

① 메마른　　　　② 비옥한

The land between the two rivers was a **fertile** one, vital for the formation of a civilization.

> 여기서 one은 앞에 있는 명사 land를 대신하는 대명사입니다.

＊ **conscience**와 역사적 지식을 지닌 사람들에게, 인종차별주의는 무지와 무감각을 나타내는 극도의 사고방식이다.

➡ .... 친 단어의 뜻은?

① 차별　　　　② 양심

> 여기서 those는 '사람들'이라는 뜻 입니다.

For those with a **conscience** and historical knowledge, racism is an extreme mindset that represents ignorance and insensitivity.

vital 필수적인, 생명의	civilization 문명	racism 인종 차별
mindset 사고방식	sensitivity 민감함	insensitivity 무감각

* 자연환경에 노출되면 어린이들의 **reasoning**과 관찰능력이 향상됩니다.

➡ .... 친 단어의 뜻은?
  ① 무지, 무식   ② 추리, 논리

> Exposure to natural environments also improves children's
> **reasoning** and observational skills.

* 또한 **mandatory** 숙려(진정시키는)기간도 사람들에게 숙고할 시간을 줌으
  로써 이혼을 줄이는 것을 도왔다.

➡ .... 친 단어의 뜻은?
  ① 자발적인   ② 의무적인

> Also the **mandatory** cooling—off period had helped reduce
> divorces by giving people time for reflection.

exposure 노출   observational 관찰의   cool off 진정시키다
reduce 줄이다   reflection 숙고, 반영, 반사

152

TEST 33 복습

▶ 단어 연결하기

skepticism	무감각
phenomenon	숙고, 반성, 반사
corporation	양심
lay off	회의론
employee	형성
fertile	회사
vital	의무적인
formation	현상
conscience	비옥한
racism	추리, 논리
insensitivity	(일시적으로) 해고하다
exposure	노출
reasoning	인종차별주의
mandatory	종업원, 직원
reflection	필수적인, 생명과 관련된

▶ ___ 채우기

최소한 ➡ at _____

사람들에게 숙고할 시간을 줌으로써

➡ ___ giving people time _____ reflection

153

* **Unparalleled** 풍년 때문에 쌀(값)이 똥값으로 떨어졌다.

➡ .... 친 단어의 뜻은?
   ① 조촐한   ② 유례없는

> Due to the **unparalleled** good harvest, the rice dropped to a
> dirt cheap price.

* 모직천이나 머리카락에 풍선을 비비면 **static electricity**가 발생한다.

➡ .... 친 단어의 뜻은?
   ① 냄새   ② 정전기

> Rubbing the balloons against woolen fabric or hair creates
> **static electricity**.

---

harvest **수확**   dirt **먼지, 값어치 없는 것**   rub **비비다**   fabric **천, 직물**
static **정적인, 정지된**

* 한국 여자 양궁 선수들은 **unbeatable**이다.

➡ .... 친 단어의 뜻은?
① 천하태평인   ② 천하무적인

Korean women archers are **unbeatable**.

> beat(이기다), beatable(이길 수 있는),
> unbeatable(이길 수 없는, 천하무적인)

* 엔진에 심각한 문제가 있어서 **mechanic**은 수리하기 위해 그것을 분해해야 했다.

➡ .... 친 단어의 뜻은?
① 검사   ② 정비사

The engine had a serious problem, so the **mechanic** had to take it apart in order to fix it.

archer 궁수, 양궁선수   serious 심각한   take apart 분해하다

＊ **Contagion**으로부터의 최고의 예방은 손을 자주 씻는 것이다.

➡ .... 친 단어의 뜻은?
  ① 더러움   ② 감염

> The best prevention from **contagion** is washing your hands often.

＊ 해킹은 강탈하고 **manipulate**하고 또는 훔치기 위해 한 개인의 전문지식을 사용하는 것과 같다.

➡ .... 친 단어의 뜻은?
  ① 조언하다.   ② 조작하다.

> equivalent는 '동등한'이고 be equivalent to ~ing는 '~와 같다'입니다.
> 그런데 to 다음에는 보통 동사원형이 많이 오는데
> 위 구문에서는 동명사(~ing)가 오는 것이 주의합시다.

> Hacking is equivalent to using one's expertise to extort, **manipulate** or steal.

prevention 예방   expertise 전문지식   extort 강탈하다

156

TEST 34 복습

▶ 단어 연결하기

unparalleled	•	• 조작하다
harvest	•	• 예방
rub	•	• 동등한
fabric	•	• 유례없는
static electricity	•	• 정전기
archer	•	• 강탈하다, 갈취하다
unbeatable	•	• 천, 직물
mechanic	•	• 수확
prevention	•	• 전문지식
contagion	•	• 기계공, 정비사
equivalent	•	• 감염
expertise	•	• 양궁선수
extort	•	• 천하무적인, 이길 수 없는
manipulate	•	• 비비다

▶ ___ 채우기

그것을 분해해야 했다 ➡ had to _____ it _____

한 개인의 전문지식을 사용하는 것과 같다

        ➡ is _____ to_____ one's expertise

STEP 35

* **Aspirations**는 희망과 꿈에서부터 나오며 오로지 헌신적인 사람만이 이룰 수 있다.

➜ .... 친 단어의 뜻은?
   ① 원망   ② 열망

> **Aspirations** come from hopes and dreams and only a dedicated person can accomplish them.

* 이동통신과 PC 시장의 스티브 잡스처럼 산업의 어떤 분야라도 **pioneer**는 항상 존재한다.

➜ .... 친 단어의 뜻은?
   ① 불구자   ② 선구자

> There always exists a **pioneer** in any field of industry, just like Steve Jobs in the mobile and PC markets.

accomplish 성취하다   exist 존재하다

＊ **Pessimists**는 세상의 종말이 곧 발생할 것이라고 믿었다.

➡ .... 친 단어의 뜻은?
① 낙관론자 　　② 비관론자

Pessimists believed the end of the world would come to pass soon.

＊ 유연한 **spine**과 길고 얇은 다리, 큰 폐, 확장된 심장 덕분에 치타는 단 몇 초 만에 0에서 시속 110km까지 가속할 수 있습니다.

➡ .... 친 단어의 뜻은?
① 턱 　　② 척추

A cheetah can also accelerate from 0 to 110km per hour in just a few seconds thanks to a flexible **spine**, long thin legs, large lungs and an enlarged heart.

come to pass 발생하다(=happen)　　flexible 유연한　　enlarge 확장하다
enlarged 확장된

＊ 기내 안전띠 표시등이 켜져 있고 **turbulence**가 있을 때 한 승객이 화장실에 가고 싶어 한다면 어떻게 할 건가요?

➜ .... 친 단어의 뜻은?
  ① 제트기류　　　　② 난기류

What would you do if a passenger wants to go to the toilet, when the in-flight seat belt sign is on and there is **turbulence**?

＊ 어느 누구도 남북한간의 군사적 **clash** 가능성을 배제할 수 없다.

➜ .... 친 단어의 뜻은?
  ① 충성　　　　② 충돌

No one can rule out the possibility of a military **clash** between the South and the North.

passenger 승객　　　in-flight 비행 중, 기내의　　　rule out 배제하다, 제외하다
military 군사적

160

TEST 35 복습

▶ 단어 연결하기

aspiration •	• 발생하다
dedicated •	• 충돌(하다)
accomplish •	• 비관론자
pioneer •	• 열망
industry •	• 척추
pessimist •	• 헌신적인
come to pass •	• 가능성
accelerate •	• 난기류, 소동
flexible •	• 이루다, 성취하다
spine •	• 승객
enlarge •	• 선구자
passenger •	• 산업
turbulence •	• 가속하다
possibility •	• 유연한
clash •	• 확장하다

▶ ___ 채우기

0에서 시속 110km까지 ➡ _____ 0 to 110km _____ hour

어느 누구도 배제할 수 없다 ➡ _____ one can rule _____

STEP 31

+ Diplomats should be proficient in English, as it is the global language used around the world.

+ Pneumonia is an infection or inflammation of the lungs.

+ Last year, 140,000 traffic accidents occurred due to negligence in keeping eyes forward, accounting for 63 percent of all traffic accidents.

+ People who don't study history are prone to bad historical analogies.

+ Snake bites literally paralyze the animal victim to allow the snake to swallow it slowly.

+ Three man and a six-year-old girl are safe now after being rescued from their tiny boat which had been adrift in the Gulf of Mexico for two days.

STEP 32

+ The store can give you a full refund provided you show us the original receipt.

+ The new charger is compatible with almost all types of cell phones in the market.

+ Mark, who was excellent at math, astronomy and physics, was interested in computer programming as a child.

+ Fast food is deficient in essential nutrients.

+ Thunder and lightning occur at roughly the same time, although you see the flash of lightning before you hear the thunder.

+ Picasso was a prolific artist who left thousands of works of art as his legacy.

STEP 33

+ Despite growing skepticism, the phenomenon known as the Korean Wave might be longer than expected, at least in the fashion and cosmetics industries.

+ It is very difficult for French corporations to lay off or fire employees.

+ The land between the two rivers was a fertile one, vital for the formation of a civilization.

+ For those with a conscience and historical knowledge, racism is an extreme mindset that represents ignorance and insensitivity.

+ Exposure to natural environments also improves children's reasoning and observational skills.

+ Also the mandatory cooling-off period had helped reduce divorces by giving people time for reflection.

STEP 34

+ Due to the unparalleled good harvest, the rice dropped to a dirt cheap price.

+ Rubbing the balloons against woolen fabric or hair creates static electricity.

+ Korean women archers are unbeatable.

+ The engine had a serious problem, so the mechanic had to take it apart in order to fix it.

+ The best prevention from contagion is washing your hands often.

+ Hacking is equivalent to using one's expertise to extort, manipulate or steal.

STEP 35

+ Aspirations come from hopes and dreams and only a dedicated person can accomplish them.

+ There always exists a pioneer in any field of industry, just like Steve Jobs in the mobile and PC markets.

+ Pessimists believed the end of the world would come to pass soon.

+ A cheetah can also accelerate from 0 to 110km per hour in just a few seconds thanks to a flexible spine, long thin legs, large lungs and an enlarged heart.

+ What would you do if a passenger wants to go to the toilet, when the in-flight seat belt sign is on and there is turbulence?

+ No one can rule out the possibility of a military clash between the South and the North.

STEP 36

* 매력은 반투명합니다. 투명한 것도 아니고 **opaque**한 것도 아닙니다.

➡ .... 친 단어의 뜻은?
① 투명한 　　　　② 불투명한

Glamour is translucent — not transparent, not **opaque**.

* 부패방지 감시기구는 사회가 좀 더 **transparent**하게 만들기 위해 교육 프로그램을 만들 것을 계획하고 있다.

➡ .... 친 단어의 뜻은?
① 불투명한 　　　　② 투명한

Anti—corruption watchdogs plan on creating education programs to make society more **transparent**.

---

translucent **반투명한**　　　corruption **부패**　　　watchdog **감시기구, 감시견, 감시인**

* 삶과 죽음이 모두 자연의 한 조각이 아니겠는가! 그것은 모두 **fate**이다.

➡ .... 친 단어의 뜻은?
　① 운　　　　　　② 운명

Both life and death are just a part of nature ! It's all **fate**.

* 일본은 한글 사용을 금지했고 한국의 역사를 **distorted**.

➡ .... 친 단어의 뜻은?
　① 찬양했다.　　　　② 왜곡했다.

Japan banned the Korean language and **distorted** Korean history.

death 죽음　　ban 금지하다

* 설상가상으로 올해 황사는 방사능 물질을 포함하는 것으로 발견되었고 그것은 일본의 원자력 발전소에서 **have been leaked**.

➡ .... 친 단어의 뜻은?
① 노출되었다.   ② 누출되었다.

To make matters worse, this year's yellow dust is found to contain radioactive materials, which **have been leaked** from nuclear power plants in Japan.

* 모기들은 특히 습하고 **damp** 지역에서 매우 빠르게 번식한다.

➡ .... 친 단어의 뜻은?
① 평온한   ② 축축한

Mosquitoes reproduce very quickly especially in humid and **damp** areas.

radioactive 방사능의   plant 공장, 식물, 심다   reproduce 번식하다, 복제하다
humid 습한, 습기가 많은

TEST 36 복습

▶ **단어 연결하기**

transparent •	• 축축한
opaque •	• 먼지
corruption •	• 왜곡하다
death •	• 불투명한
fate •	• 번식하다
ban •	• 금지하다
distort •	• 누출(하다)
dust •	• 투명한
radioactive •	• 부패
leak •	• 죽음
mosquito •	• 모기
reproduce •	• 방사능을 가진
damp •	• 운명

▶ **＿＿ 채우기**

설상가상으로 ➡ to make matters ＿＿＿＿＿＿

* 최근에 서울시 정부는 서울의 호텔, 모텔 78개의 업체에 대해 무작위로 **sanitary** 검사를 실시했다.

➡ .... 친 단어의 뜻은?
   ① 숙제   ② 위생(의)

Recently, the Seoul Metropolitan Government conducted random **sanitary** tests on 78 hotels and motels in Seoul.

* 대부분의 십대들은 **puberty**와 함께 오는 호르몬의 변화들 때문에 여드름이 나게 된다.

➡ .... 친 단어의 뜻은?
   ① 갱년기   ② 사춘기

Most teens get pimples because of the hormonal changes that come with **puberty**.

---

metropolitan **대도시의**   random **무작위의**   pimple **여드름**

* 이 드라마는 현재 KBS에서 방송되고 있으며, 화려한 출연진과 **intriguing** 이야기로 팬들로부터 인기를 끌고 있다.

➡ .... 친 단어의 뜻은?
   ① 단조로운   ② 흥미로운

> The drama is currently airing on KBS, and has been popular among fans due to its gorgeous cast and **intriguing** story.

* 첫번째로 지구는 equator라고 불리는 가상의 선에 의해 반으로 나뉜다.

➡ .... 친 단어의 뜻은?
   ① 경도   ② 적도

> First, Earth is divided in half by an imaginary line called the equator.

---

currently 현재   air 방송하다, 공기   gorgeous 화려한, 멋진
imaginary 가상의

* 해외유학의 열풍은 서울의 남쪽지방인 **affluent** 강남에서 시작됐다.

➡ .... 친 단어의 뜻은?
① 초라한 ② 부유한

> The craze over studying abroad started in the **affluent** Gangnam area in southern Seoul.

* 위키리크스의 목적은 **anonymous** 제보자로부터 받은 기밀정보를 공개하는 것이다.

➡ .... 친 단어의 뜻은?
① 우수한 ② 익명의

> WikiLeaks' goal is to unveil secret information from **anonymous** sources.

---

craze **열풍, 미치다**　　　unveil **공개하다, 드러내다**　　　source **제보자, 원천**

TEST 37 복습

▶ 단어 연결하기

random •		• 부유한, 풍부한
sanitary •		• 화려한, 멋진
currently •		• 무작위의
gorgeous •		• 익명의
intriguing •		• 공개하다, 베일을 벗기다
equator •		• 위생의
pimple •		• 사춘기
puberty •		• 적도
affluent •		• 현재
unveil •		• 흥미로운
anonymous •		• 여드름

▶ ___ 채우기

적도라고 불리는 ➡ _____ the equator

* **Precipitation**의 총량은 예년과 비슷하지만 짧은 시간에 집중적으로 쏟아
지는 폭우가 홍수 위험을 높인다.

➡ .... 친 단어의 뜻은?
① 우산   ② 강우, 강수(량)

> The total amount of **precipitation** was similar to normal years,
> but a lot of rains in a short period of time increased the danger
> of flooding.

* 공정거래법은 어떤 매체를 통해서든 부당하고 **deceptive** 광고를 금하고
있다.

➡ .... 친 단어의 뜻은?
① 야한   ② 기만적인, 속이는

> The fair trade law prohibits unfair or **deceptive** advertising in
> any medium.

---

normal **일반적인, 정상인**   prohibit **금하다**

172

* 비옥한 땅으로부터 원주민들을 **to banish** 그들은 무력을 썼다.

➡ .... 친 단어의 뜻은?
① 초대하기 위해   ② 추방하기 위해

They used force **to banish** the natives from the fertile land.

* 많은 시민들이 **tyranny**에 대한 저항의 표시로 **촛불을 밝혔다.**

➡ .... 친 단어의 뜻은?
① 무능   ② 폭정, 독재

Many citizens lit candles as a show of resistance **against the tyranny.**

---

fertile **비옥한**   resistance **저항**

* 주로 눈 주위와 얼굴 부위에 이 독성물질이 주입되면, 얼굴 근육을 풀어주고 주름이 생기는 것을 <u>lessens</u>.

➡ .... 친 단어의 뜻은?
   ① 방치한다.   ② 줄인다.

> When this toxin is injected, usually around the eyes and face area, it relaxes the facial muscles and <u>lessens</u> the appearance of wrinkles.

* 한국식품안전청은 금요일에 일부 중국산 김치에서 **parasite** 알이 발견되어 회수하여 폐기할 것을 지시했다고 발표했다.

➡ .... 친 단어의 뜻은?
   ① 거북이   ② 기생충

> The Korea Food and Drug Administration announced Friday that some Chinese kimchi contains **parasite** eggs and ordered that it be recalled and destroyed.

주장, 제안, 요구 동사 뒤 that 절에는 조동사 should가 생략될 수 있습니다.
그래서 동사원형 be가 사용되고 있습니다.

appearance 출현   recall 회수하다, 상기하다   destroy 파괴하다

TEST 38 복습

▶ 단어 연결하기

precipitation •		• 강우, 강수(량)
similar •		• 줄이다
flooding •		• 폭정, 독재
prohibit •		• 금지하다
deceptive •		• 비슷한
banish •		• 기생충
fertile •		• 발표하다
resistance •		• 홍수
tyranny •		• 비옥한
toxin •		• 기만적인, 속이는
inject •		• 저항
lessen •		• 독성물질
wrinkle •		• 주입하다
announce •		• 주름
parasite •		• 추방하다

▶ ___ 채우기

저항의 표시로 ➜ ___ a show of resistance

이 독성물질이 주입되면 ➜ when this _____ ___ injected

STEP 39

* 블레어는 여동생을 때린 이유로 어머니로부터 **was reproached.**

   → .... 친 단어의 뜻은?
   ① 용돈을 받았다.   ② 꾸지람을 받았다.

   Blair **was reproached** by her mother for hitting her sister.

* 직독직해 부메랑 / 주인에 의해 던져진 / 새들을 떨어뜨렸다. / 그리고 고양이는 / 그것들을 **would retrieve.**

   → .... 친 단어의 뜻은?
   ① 요리하곤 했다.   ② 회수하곤 했다.

   > fling(던지다)의 과거분사입니다.

   A boomerang / flung by the master / brought the birds down / and the cat / **would retrieve them.**

---

reproach 꾸짖다, 비난하다   retrieve 회수하다

176

* 그들은 왜 직원들이 정기적으로 쉬어야 하는지를 설명하는 **leaflets**와 스티커를 나누어주고 있다.

➡ .... 친 단어의 뜻은?
① 건전지   ② 전단지

They have been handing out **leaflets** and stickers that explain why employees need to take regular breaks.

* 그녀는 **plague**로 고생했다(괴롭힘을 당해왔다).

➡ .... 친 단어의 뜻은?
① 술병   ② 전염병

She has been plagued **by the plague**.

---

hand out **나누어 주다**   break **휴식, 깨뜨리다**   plague **전염병, 괴롭히다**

* 또한 **capitalist** 사회에서 미디어는 때때로 돈이나 권력 같은 다른 요인들에 의해 조종당하기도 한다.

➡ .... 친 단어의 뜻은?
  ① 채무자   ② 자본가

> Also, media is sometimes controlled by other factors such as money and power in **capitalist** societies.

* 결국 서울시 유권자들은 모든 학생들에게 무상 급식을 제공해야 할지, 점진적으로 그 정책을 **implement**해야 할지를 결정할 것이다.

➡ .... 친 단어의 뜻은?
  ① 폐지하다.   ② 시행하다.

> Seoul city's voters will ultimately decide whether to provide free lunch to all students or **implement** the policy on a gradual basis.

---

factor **요소**   ultimately **결국**   policy **정책**   gradual **점진적인**

TEST 39 복습

▶ 단어 연결하기

reproach •	• 직원
flung •	• 전염병, 괴롭히다
retrieve •	• 투표자
leaflet •	• 정책
explain •	• 시행하다
employee •	• 꾸짖다, 비난하다
plague •	• 설명하다
factor •	• 결국, 궁극적으로
capitalist •	• 던져진
voter •	• 회수하다
ultimately •	• 자본가
implement •	• 요소
policy •	• 전단지

▶ ___ 채우기

주인에 의해 던져진 ➡ _____ by the master

괴롭힘을 당해왔다 ➡ has been _____

점진적으로 ➡ on a _____ basis

* 에티오피아는 **famine**으로 고통 받는 나라인데도 헝거씨는 그곳에서 소화제를 팔려고 한다.

➡ .... 친 단어의 뜻은?
① 추위　　　　② 기근, 기아

> Ethiopia is a country afflicted by **famine** and Mr. Hunger is going to sell digestives there.

* 무역회담의 중요성을 고려하여 150명의 한국 **delegates**는 지금 브뤼셀에서 관련된 임무를 수행 중이다.

➡ .... 친 단어의 뜻은?
① 선수(단)　　　② 대표 (단)

> given은 전치사로 사용되기도 합니다.
> (~를 고려하면)이라고 해석됩니다.

> Given the importance of the trade talks, some 150 Koreans **delegates** are now on relevant mission in Brussels

afflict 괴롭히다, 고통을 주다　　　digestive 소화제, 소화의　　　relevant 관련된

＊ 난 책상에 너무 오랜 시간 동안 앉아 있어서 목과 어깨가 **stiff**하다.

➡ .... 친 단어의 뜻은?
① 간지러운　　　② 뻣뻣한

I'm sitting such long hours at my desk that my neck and shoulders are **stiff**.

<such 명사 … that 주어 동사 ~> 구문입니다.
<너무 … 해서 ~하다>로 해석됩니다.

＊ 고용주는 여전히 당신의 다음 달 급여를 지불할 **liable**이 있다.

➡ .... 친 단어의 뜻은?
① 권리가 있는　　　② 책임이 있는

The employer is still **liable** to pay your next month's salary.

employer **고용주**　　salary **봉급**

* 정부는 어제 공교육을 <u>by fortifying</u> 사교육비를 경감시키기 위한 계획을 발표했다.

➡ .... 친 단어의 뜻은?
  ① 강조함으로써   ② 강화함으로써

> The government yesterday released plans to cut private tutoring costs **by fortifying** the public education system.

* 토론자들이 근거 없는 주장을 할 때 이러한 **fallacy**를 범하게 된다.

➡ .... 친 단어의 뜻은?
  ① 정당성   ② 오류

> Debaters commit this **fallacy** when they make an unfounded claim.

> found(기초를 쌓다, 설립하다)의 과거분사인
> founded(~에 기초한) / unfounded: 기초가 없는, 근거 없는

---

private 사적인, 개인의   fortify 강화하다   debater 토론자
claim 주장(하다)

TEST 40 복습

▶ **단어 연결하기**

afflict	고용주
famine	뻣뻣한
digestive	임무
delegate	관련된
relevant	대표(단)
mission	소화제, 소화의
stiff	기근, 기아
employer	괴롭히다, 고통을 주다
liable	책임 있는
private	근거 없는
fortify	사적인, 개인의
fallacy	강화하다
unfounded	오류

▶ **___ 채우기**

기근으로 고통 받는 ➡ _____ by famine

근거 없는 주장 ➡ _____ claim

STEP 36~40 묶음해석 연습

STEP 36

+ Glamour is translucent – not transparent, not opaque.
+ Anti-corruption watchdogs plan on creating education programs to make society more transparent.
+ Both life and death are just a part of nature! It's all fate.
+ Japan banned the Korean language and distorted Korean history.
+ To make matters worse, this year's yellow dust is found to contain radioactive materials, which have been leaked from nuclear power plants in Japan.
+ Mosquitoes reproduce very quickly especially in humid and damp areas.

STEP 37

+ Recently, the Seoul Metropolitan Government conducted random sanitary tests on 78 hotels and motels in Seoul.
+ Most teens get pimples because of the hormonal changes that come with puberty.
+ The drama is currently airing on KBS, and has been popular among fans due to its gorgeous cast and intriguing story.
+ First, Earth is divided in half by an imaginary line called the equator.
+ The craze over studying abroad started in the affluent Gangnam area in southern Seoul.
+ WikiLeaks' goal is to unveil secret information from anonymous sources.

STEP 38

+ The total amount of precipitation was similar to normal years, but a lot of rains in a short period of time increased the danger of flooding.
+ The fair trade law prohibits unfair or deceptive advertising in any medium.
+ They used force to banish the natives from the fertile land.
+ Many citizens lit candles as a show of resistance against the tyranny.

+ When this toxin is injected, usually around the eyes and face area, it relaxes the facial muscles and lessens the appearance of wrinkles.
+ The Korea Food and Drug Administration announced Friday that some Chinese kimchi contains parasite eggs and ordered that it be recalled and destroyed.

STEP 39

+ Blair was reproached by her mother for hitting her sister.
+ A boomerang flung by the master brought the birds down and the cat would retrieve them.
+ They have been handing out leaflets and stickers that explain why employees need to take regular breaks.
+ She has been plagued by the plague.
+ Also, media is sometimes controlled by other factors such as money and power in capitalist societies.
+ Seoul city's voters will ultimately decide whether to provide free lunch to all students or implement the policy on a gradual basis.

STEP 40

+ Ethiopia is a country afflicted by famine and Mr. Hunger is going to sell digestives there.
+ Given the importance of the trade talks, some 150 Koreans delegates are now on relevant mission in Brussels.
+ I'm sitting such long hours at my desk that my neck and shoulders are stiff.
+ The employer is still liable to pay your next month's salary.
+ The government yesterday released plans to cut private tutoring costs by fortifying the public education system.
+ Debaters commit this fallacy when they make an unfounded claim.

이²번이 정답인
수능기본
영단어 영문장

초판 1쇄 2015년 09월 25일

지은이 성근모
발행인 김재홍
디자인 박선경, 박상아, 이슬기
마케팅 이연실

발행처 도서출판 지식공감
등록번호 제396-2012-000018호
주소 경기도 고양시 일산동구 견달산로225번길 112
전화 02-3141-2700
팩스 02-322-3089
홈페이지 www.bookdaum.com

가격 12,000원
ISBN 979-11-5622-119-7 53740